THE TWENTIETH-CENTURY STRING QUARTET

THE
TWENTIETH-CENTURY
STRING
QUARTET

Edited by
Douglas Jarman

RNCM
ROYAL NORTHERN
COLLEGE OF MUSIC
in association with

MUSIC
2002

Published by Arc Music
Nanholme Mill, Shaw Wood Road
Todmorden, Lancs OL14 6DA

Design by Tony Ward
Printed at the Arc & Throstle Press
Nanholme Mill, Todmorden, Lancs, UK

ISBN 1 900072 56 4

ACKNOWLEDGEMENTS
The musical examples throughout the text are repro-
duced by kind permission of Boosey & Hawkes,
Deshon Music & PMW Editions, Peters Edition,
London and Universal Edition.

The publishers wish to thank the Principal of the
RNCM and Dr. Christopher Rowland, Director of
Chamber Music at the RNCM for their invaluable
support for this project.

Contents

Editor's Preface

The following book has its origins in a festival devoted to the twentieth-century string quartet that took place at the Royal Northern College of Music, Manchester, in January 2000, the first month of the twenty-first century and also the month that (despite the arguments of purists) was popularly accepted as being the first of the new millennium. Although it was impossible to perform all the important string quartets written in the twentieth century in the course of the four day festival, over ninety of the most significant were played, alongside a number of premieres of works written in the closing months of the century which had been especially commissioned for the festival from young composers.

It is, I think, fair to say that for those of us that attended what became known as the QuartetFest, one of the most remarkable and unanticipated results of four days of listening only to quartets written during the course of the twentieth century was the degree to which our ears and minds adapted to the musical idiom, so that by the final concert, the language of the quartets of Carter or Ferneyhough had become as approachable as that of Bartók or Janáček.

But perhaps the most important achievement of this extraordinary festival was the extent to which it demonstrated that the string quartet not only remains, even after two hundred and fifty years, a vital and developing genre, but also that it is still the medium which makes the greatest demands on a composer's technical skills and a vehicle for the most concentrated, the most experimental and the most radical – as well as the most intimate – compositional thought.

In tandem with the concerts ran a series of lectures by eminent composers, performers and musicologists in which were considered such topics as the development of the quartet genre during the course of the century, new performance techniques and the legacy of historic recordings. These lectures form the basis of the present book.

The majority of the QuartetFest lectures were concerned with the development of the string quartet within particular national or geographic areas and this method of organisation has been maintained in the present volume. Inevitably, certain countries and composers have fallen through the net – there is, for example, little on Australian or Scandinavian contributions to the medium – but, if not totally inclusive, the scope of the book is, I believe, nonetheless relatively comprehensive. Although the QuartetFest lectures have been rewritten in such a way that they read as self-sufficient chapters, independent of the festival itself, there has been no attempt to arrive at a common format or to impose a common style. Hopefully the reader will find the widely differing approaches and viewpoints of the various contributors both refreshing and a reflection of the multi-faceted richness of the subject.

My thanks are due to all the authors involved, but especially to Dr. Caroline Potter and Dr. Amanda Bayley who, when two of the speakers who took part in the festival found themselves unable to contribute to the book, kindly agreed to deal with the two important areas which were consequently left undiscussed.

Thanks are also due to Dr. Christopher Rowland, Director of Chamber Music at the RNCM who, as Artistic Director of the QuartetFest, organised the four-day event.

Since many of the works discussed are still in copyright, only essential musical examples have been included. Elsewhere, passages of music that are specifically mentioned in the text are indicated either by bar numbers, or by reference to the rehearsal figures in the score. Editions are not specified since most of the works discussed are only available in one edition.

Douglas Jarman
January 2002

I
The Austro-German Quartet

Douglas Jarman

To many of the most 'forward looking' composers of the second half of the nineteenth century, the string quartet was a medium that no longer served their expressive needs; the development of instrumental technology – which afforded the possibility of vast orchestral canvases and large-scale rhetorical effects of a kind that had been previously undreamed of – and the fashion for programme music had tempted composers such as Liszt and Wagner to turn elsewhere.

In the middle of the nineteenth century, the German musical world had been split, bitterly and vociferously, between those who believed in music as a pure autonomous art (the Brahmsians, led by the critic Eduard Hanslick) and those interested in it as an art that was dependent on literature or drama (the Wagnerians and the devotees of programme music of the kind represented by Liszt and later Strauss). In this fight between the 'traditionalists' and the 'radicals', it was the conservatives who continued to write chamber music and abstract, non-programmatic forms such as the symphony. The young advanced composers tended to write in more radical forms: music dramas, programmatic symphonies and symphonic poems. The Brahms-Wagner controversy gradually died down but even so, by the late 1880s and 1890s, many of the most important Austrian and German composers, such as Mahler and Strauss, showed little interest in the string quartet.

What is most striking in the early years of the twentieth century is the revival of interest in the genre by the generation that followed Mahler and Strauss. The last few years of the nineteenth and the first thirty-three years of the twentieth centuries saw the composition not only of the works of the Second Viennese School – three quartets by Arnold Schoenberg (1874-1951), or four if we include the early and uncharacteristic D major Quartet,[1] two by Alban Berg (1885-1935), the *Five Movements* op. 5 and the *Baga-*

---

[1] The D major Quartet (1897) remained unpublished during Schoenberg's lifetime and received its first performances only in 1966.

telles op. 9 in addition to the op. 28 Quartet of Anton Webern
(1883-1945) – but also four quartets by Zemlinsky, five by Reger,
two by Krenek, four by Hindemith, two by Weill, two by Korngold
and numerous others by composers like Schullhoff, Ullmann, Karl
Weigl and Egon Wellesz.

Of course, some of these string quartets were student works.
Writing such pieces – sets of variations for piano, then for string
quartet, followed by the composition of more complex forms such
as piano sonatas and string quartet movements – was still an accepted part of a young composer's training. There are, for example, six abandoned piano sonatas and dozens of short string quartet pieces by Berg and a number of string quartet movements, or
fragments of movements, by Webern written while they were studying with Schoenberg. Similarly, the early string quartet by Krenek
was written when he was finishing his studies with Schreker and
the quartet movements by T. W. Adorno during his years as a
composition student under Berg. The Quartet in B minor of Kurt
Weill (1900-1950), which dates from his years with Busoni, is no
more indicative of the interests of the mature Weill than is the
single chamber work, a piano quartet, by Mahler indicative of the
future work of that composer. Nonetheless, there remains a substantial body of chamber music written by Austro-German composers in the first third of the twentieth century.

How are we to account for this recurrence of interest in a genre that
had been almost ignored by the previous generation of composers?

In the period following the First World War, the reappearance
of the string quartet and other Classical forms in the output of a
composer such as Paul Hindemith (1895-1963) may be taken as a
symptom of the fashionable belief in a cooler, more Classical objectivity and in the necessity for creating functional, practical works.
Hindemith, a skilled professional viola player, wrote his first four
string quartets for performance by his own quartet – the First Quartet of 1918 was written when he was playing in a quartet in the
course of doing military service, while nos. 2-4 were all written in
1922-3 when he was a member of the newly-formed Amar Quartet.

More interesting in terms of their *raison d'être* are those quartets
by composers who, whether through age or inclination, were unaffected by the 'New Objectivity' [*Neue Sachlichkeit*] which characterised much German and Austrian music in the inter-war period.

The works of Max Reger (1837-1916), born a generation be-

fore Hindemith, in some ways typify the dichotomy which faced
the Austro-German composer of the late nineteenth and early
twentieth century. Unable to ignore the overpowering influence
of the harmonic and melodic language of Wagner, Reger had, nonetheless, a natural sympathy for the Classical formal ideals of Brahms
(and, as an organist, with the technique of Bach), and consciously
chose to align himself with the traditionalists: "Even if Lessmann
[the editor of the *Allgemeine Musik-Zeitung*] takes such pains to
disperse Brahms and the Brahms fog, the Brahms fog will remain.
And I much prefer it to the white heat of Wagner and Strauss"[2],
wrote Reger to his friend Adalbert Linder in 1894. It is significant
that Schoenberg, who was equally eager to link himself to the
Brahmsian tradition, rated Reger highly and ensured that his works
were a regular feature of the programmes of the Society for Private
Musical Performances.

Equally symptomatic is the case of Alexander von Zemlinsky
(1872-1942), whose four quartets – the first written in 1896 and
the last in 1936 – cover most of his creative life. Zemlinsky had
been taught by Brahms enthusiasts at the Vienna Conservatory
and his First Quartet is unashamedly Brahmsian in material, treatment and form (even to the extent that its two central movements are, as so often in Brahms, 'character pieces' rather than
true scherzo and slow movements). The year before composing
the quartet, Zemlinsky had met not only Brahms himself but had
also met and become friends with (and would later become the
brother-in-law of) the young Schoenberg who played cello in the
amateur PolyHymnia orchestra that Zemlinsky conducted. At the
time of meeting, Schoenberg was writing his own early, and also
Brahmsian, D major Quartet. By the time Zemlinsky came to write
his Second Quartet (1913-15), however, Schoenberg had produced two works which were to have a lasting influence on Zemlinsky: the string sextet *Verklärte Nacht* and the work that he ac-
knowledged as his first string quartet, the D minor Quartet op 7.
The influence of these epoch-making works is immediately evident in both the language and structure of Zemlinsky's Second
Quartet which, like Schoenberg's op. 7, adopts an intricate single

[2] Quoted in Frisch, Walter, *The Early Works of Arnold Schoenberg, 1893-1908* (Berkeley:
University of California Press, 1993), p. 3.

movement structure and, like both *Verklärte Nacht* and op. 7, ends with a glowing major-key apotheosis.

Happily the music of Zemlinsky, who died a forgotten figure in New York, has enjoyed something of a renaissance in the last twenty years, largely due to performances of the operas which are, arguably, his most important works. The music of Zemlinsky's pupil, Karl Weigl (1881-1949) – whom Schoenberg described as "one of the best composers of the old school" – has unfortunately not yet attracted the attention which it deserves, although the eight quartets and in particular the First Quartet in C minor, completed a year before Schoenberg's First Quartet, would be a valuable addition to the repertoire of any ensemble.

The importance that the string quartet (along with other traditional genres like the *Klavierstück* and the concerto) assumes in the work of Schoenberg, Berg and Webern, illustrates the conflict of traditions which the Austro-German composer of the generation after Mahler and Strauss had to reconcile. In the works of the Second Viennese School, the quartet – the genre that the 'forward-looking' composers of the previous generation had rejected as old-fashioned – lies at the heart of one of the most radical changes in the nature of the musical language, and the string quartet in particular becomes the vehicle for the most revolutionary experiments in language, form and texture.

Thus, each of the first three string quartets of Schoenberg stands at a significant point in the development of his musical language; the *Five Movements for String Quartet* op. 5, and even more the tiny *Bagatelles* op. 9 of Webern, explore a completely new world of structure and timbre (and of structure as defined by timbre), while in the *Lyric Suite*, Berg produced a work of such a stature that its influence would be felt for the rest of the century.

There are many reasons for this apparent paradoxical yoking of traditional genre and radical thought. Living in the city of Haydn, Mozart, Beethoven and Brahms – the late quartets of Beethoven had already established the string quartet as a forum for formal and textural innovation – the three composers of the Second Viennese School were deeply aware of both the weight of, and their place in, the Viennese musical tradition.

In the case of Schoenberg and Berg, it is not too fanciful to suggest that the sense of having to stake a claim as descendants of this great tradition was also compounded by personal factors, since both composers were trained outside those musical institutions – the Hochschule für Musik, the Vienna Academy and the University – that were regarded as embodying that tradition.[3] Apart from a few sessions with Zemlinsky, Schoenberg was an autodiktat while Berg (whose school career had been so disastrous that he would not, in any case, have had the entry qualifications demanded by such august institutions) was, until he went to Schoenberg, essentially a dilettante who remained painfully aware of his lack of formal training and his consequent technical deficiencies for many years. Of the three composers of the Second Viennese School only Webern, who had studied as a musicologist under Guido Adler at the University, had had a formal training that would have been recognised by the Viennese musical establishment.

To Schoenberg, Berg and Webern, their musical language – and the step from tonality to atonality – was the inevitable and logical outcome of the Austro-German tradition: as Webern said, "Our push forward *had* to be".[4] In the eyes of the establishment, they were destroying the very language on which that tradition was based.

Unsurprisingly, therefore, the three members of the Second Viennese School felt the need to assert their relation to tradition. Schoenberg in particular seems to have felt the need to assert it ever more pronouncedly the further he moved away from the kind of harmonies and pitch figurations of the tonal language that embodied that tradition.

The four string quartets of Schoenberg chart this development in microcosm. The First Quartet op. 7, which employs a highly chromatic, but undeniably tonal, musical language, has an extraordinarily intricate structure that fuses the traditional four-movement design into a single forty-five minute movement in which the development and recapitulation of the sonata form first movement are spread across the work thus:

---

[3] For a perceptive discussion of Schoenberg's and Berg's relation to both the Viennese musical establishment and the Classical tradition, see Hailey, Christopher, 'Berg and the Viennese Dichotomy' in Jarman, Douglas (ed.), *The Berg Companion* (London: Macmillan, 1989), pp. 221-234.

[4] Webern, Anton, *The Path to New Music* (Pennsylvania: Theodor Presser and Co., 1963), p. 45.

Mvt. 1	Mvt. 1	Mvt. 1	Mvt. 1
Sonata form	Development	Development	
	Recap. 1st subj.	Recap. 2nd subj.	Coda

	Mvt. 2	Mvt. 3	Mvt. 4
	Scherzo	Adagio	Finale

The whole work is held together by thematic interconnections so intricate and so numerous that there is hardly a single phrase of a single part that is not in some way thematic.

The Second Quartet, on the other hand, while tonally and texturally radical (the move from the clear F sharp minor of the opening movement to the atonality of the finale, and the introduction of a voice into a string quartet for the first time in the last two movements) is formally much more traditional. The piece still has the kind of thematic links between different movements which are the basis of the First Quartet but the intricate formal structure of the earlier quartet (and of the First Chamber Symphony) here gives way to a straightforward, standard four-movement format of sonata form, scherzo, variations, finale.

As though to emphasise its provenance even further, the Second Quartet also has two features which make direct reference to one of the key works in the great Viennese quartet tradition, the first of the op. 59 ('Rasumovsky') quartets of Beethoven. Firstly, the development section of the first movement of the Schoenberg (like that of op. 59 no. 1, the first quartet to dispense with the repeat of the exposition) starts with the main theme in the tonic, as though to repeat the exposition as in a Classical quartet;[5] secondly, the second movement scherzo of the Schoenberg starts with the solo cello playing a rhythm on a single repeated note, surely a deliberate allusion to the similar opening of the second movement scherzo of op. 59 no. 1.

Finally with the Third Quartet, one of the first of his major twelve-note works, and again with the Fourth Quartet (written not in Europe but in America), Schoenberg not only reverts to a totally Classical four-movement structure but also to the rhythmic, metric and gestural characteristics of earlier music.

[5] Keller, Hans, 'Schoenberg and the Crisis of Communication' in *The London Sinfonietta Schoenberg/Gerhard Series* (London: Sinfonietta Productions Ltd., 1973), p. 46.

To Schoenberg, as to his contemporary the music analyst Heinrich Schenker, the great canonic compositions were those of the Austro-German tradition and his chief concern in almost all his writings is to demonstrate to the outside world how his music, and his whole way of thinking about structure and continuity in music, stems directly from the works of Mozart, Beethoven and Brahms. In the words of the musicologist Christopher Hailey, "he aimed the canon in his own direction".[6]

One of the best known and most important of these writings is the 1947 article 'Brahms the Progressive' in which Schoenberg discusses, among other things, Brahms's exploitation of asymmetrical phrase structures (one of the features of Schoenberg's First Quartet to which Berg draws attention in his 1924 article 'Why is Schoenberg's Music so Difficult to Understand?') and the motivic construction of Brahms's music.[7]

To Schoenberg, the subtle handling of motivic variation, as exemplified by Brahms, was the defining characteristic of the great Austro-German tradition. Such a handling of motivic and thematic variation not only forms the basis of Schoenberg's first two quartets but lies at the heart of his conception of the twelve-note row. It was an idea stated most clearly by Webern when he compared the operations of the twelve-note row to Goethe's primaeval plant, in which

> the root is [...] no different from the stalk, the stalk no different from the leaf and the leaf no different from the flower [...] the same law applies to everything. Something that seems quite different is really the same [... and thus] the most comprehensive unity results.[8]

Indeed, in Webern's own twelve-note music, the row itself is conceived not as a melody but as a series of motivic variations; witness the structure of the note row of the Concerto op. 24 – the row most usually cited as the example of Webern's use of such isomor-

[6] See Hailey, Christopher, 'Schoenberg and the Canon; an Evolving Heritage', in Hailey, C. and Brand, J., *Constructive Dissonance* (Berkeley: University of California Press, 1997), p. 164.

[7] Schoenberg, Arnold, 'Brahms the Progressive' in *Style and Idea* (London: Faber and Faber, 1984), pp. 398-441.

[8] Webern, Anton, *op. cit.*, p. 53.

phic cells – or the row of the Quartet op. 28 which, as the following example demonstrates, divides into two halves (the second of
which is a retrograde inversion of the first), three identical
tetrachords, four similar (but not identical) trichords and six semitone dyads.

Ex. 1 The note row of Webern's Quartet op. 28

But although Schoenberg was concerned to emphasize his adherence to the Brahmsian ideal of music as an autonomous art,
programme music and the idea of music as some kind of dramatic
or literary narrative remained an equally strong part of the tradition in which the three composers of the Second Viennese School
grew up, and as much a part of their way of thinking.

Almost all of Schoenberg's important early works (*Guerrelieder*,
Verklärte Nacht, *Pelleas und Melisande*) have either overt texts or
implied texts behind them, and even those pieces that appear to
be 'pure music' often have a programme lurking somewhere in the
background. We know, for example, that the First Quartet had
such a programme behind it (one which Schoenberg admitted to,
but never revealed), as also had the Second Quartet.[9] It is significant that the move to atonality in the finale of the Second Quartet happens in a movement that has a text, a text which – through

[9] The autobiographical programme of the Second Quartet, which refers to a time of
great personal difficulty when his wife Mathilde had left him for the painter Richard
Gerstl, (hence the quotation from *Ach Du lieber Augustin' alles ist hin* – everything
has gone' in the Trio of the Scherzo movement) is outlined in Smith, Joan Allen,
Schoenberg and his School, (New York: Schirmer, 1986), pp. 174-5. The programme for
the First Quartet is discussed in Schmidt, Christian Martin, 'Schoenberg's "Very
Definite but Private" Programm zum Streichquartet op. 7' in *Bericht über den 2
Kongress der Internationalen Schoenberg-Gesellschaft* (Wien: Verlag Elisabeth Lafite,
1986), pp. 230-234.

references to feeling "the air from another planet" and "I lose myself in sounds" – acts as a legitimisation or an explanation of the
radical change of musical language.

Such programmatic thinking was an essential part of the creative make-up of even Webern, at least to the extent that many of
his pieces depicted specific places or were associated with specific
memories. The sketches for the first movement of the op. 28 Quartet, for example, bear the notes 'Korale'; 'spruce forest'; 'the source
of the brook'; 'garden at Schwabegg'.[10]

By 1909-10, however, programme music had become unfash-
ionable (even Strauss was no longer writing tone poems) and by
the end of the First War it had become totally outmoded – swept
away, with all the other trappings of Romanticism, by the 'New
Objectivity'. While the members of the Second Viennese School
were keen to proclaim their allegiance to the Brahmsian tradition,
their equal allegiance to programme music was not something that
they wanted to advertise – as Schoenberg said when tackled about
the programme of the First Quartet, "One doesn't talk about such
things nowadays" – and they went to some lengths to hide, or at
least play down, the literary or narrative elements in their music.
One extended, and convoluted, attempt to minimise the importance of the narrative, for example, is Berg's guide to Schoenberg's
Pelleas und Melisande, a substantial analysis in which he goes to
some lengths to show (not entirely convincingly) that the pieces is
in sonata form and thus as much a piece of pure music as it is a
piece of programme music.[11]

The ambivalent attitude towards programme music is perfectly
caught, although never outwardly expressed, in Schoenberg's curious 1911 essay on Liszt, in which he argues for Liszt's genius despite the fact that "he created an art form which our time necessarily regards as a mistake". Liszt's two errors, says Schoenberg, were
that "he suppressed the poet in himself by letting other poets talk
him into too much", and that he "who felt form as a formalism,
created a worse formalism because, in his forms created by intel-

[10] See Moldenhauer, Hans, *Anton von Webern*, (London: Gollancz, 1978), p. 486.
[11] See Derrick Puffett's critique of Berg's analysis in ' "Music that lingers within one"
for a Lifetime', *Music and Letters*, 76 / ii, May 1995, pp. 209-64.

lect, no living person has ever dwelled".[12]

The fusion of abstract formal design and detailed programmatic narrative finds its most intricate, and perhaps its most perfect, expression in the music of Berg – a composer who seems to have needed extra-musical (and usually highly subjective autobiographical) elements to stimulate his creative imagination, but who was able to incorporate such elements in works that are, as Stravinsky observed, amongst the most formally ingenious of the century.[13]

Berg's success as a composer of operas – works in which he tackled head-on the conflict between music as an autonomous, abstract, self-referential art and music as a literary, narrative, illustrative art (and tackled it in the genre in which the problem presents itself in its most acute form) – is directly relevant to his instrumental music in this respect. Having, in *Wozzeck*, clothed a powerful dramatic narrative in a series of pure, abstract instrumental forms (sonata forms, fugues, passacaglias, even in Act 2 a five-movement symphony), Berg then began to devise secret narratives for instrumental works, narratives that could be shaped in such a way as to produce the autonomous, abstract structures that his aesthetic required.

If *Wozzeck* moves Brahmsian ideals into the Wagnerian arena, the *Lyric Suite* adopts the opposite strategy and the string quartet becomes, in the words of Berg's pupil Adorno, "a latent opera".[14]

---

[12] Schoenberg, Arnold, 'Franz Liszt's Work and Being', *op. cit.*, p. 444. Equally interesting is Schoenberg's 1912 essay on 'The Relationship to the Text' (*ibid.* pp. 141-4) in which he deals with setting poetic texts, and so cannot avoid some discussion of the relationship between musical and literary or narrative structure. Having said that "the assumption that music summons up images of one sort or another is as widespread as only the false and the banal can be", Schoenberg cleverly resolves the whole problem by saying that having realised that there were several Schubert songs that he knew well without knowing what they were about, he had, on reading the poems, discovered that he had fully understood the real content of the poem from the song, and perhaps understood more deeply than if he had clung to the surface of the "mere thought expressed in the words". He himself, says Schoenberg, had composed many of his own songs without troubling himself in the slightest with the continuity of poetic events. "Only days later […] looking back to see what was the real poetic content of the song […] It turned out to my great astonishment that I had never done greater justice to the poet than when, guided by my first direct contact with the sound of the beginning, I divined everything that obviously and inevitably had to follow this first sound."
[13] In *Stravinsky in Conversation with Robert Craft* (Harmondsworth: Penguin, 1962), p. 86.
[14] Adorno, Theodor W., *Alban Berg*, trans. Julianne Brand and Christopher Hailey (Cambridge: Cambridge University Press, 1991), p. 104.

Like Janáček's Second Quartet, the *Lyric Suite* is a record of a doomed love affair in which the second movement (*Andante amoroso*) paints a portrait of Hanna Fuchs-Robettin, the woman with whom he was in love, and her children; the third movement (*Allegro misterioso* and *Trio estatico*) depicts their first expressions of love; and the fourth (*Adagio appassionato*) is a love scene. In the last two movements, the work spirals downward through a nightmarish scherzo (*Presto delirando*) to the final hopeless *Largo desolato*, a movement that, in the published score, is purely instrumental but which Berg composed as a setting of Stefan George's translation of *De Profundis Clamavi* from Baudelaire's *Les Fleurs du mal*. Berg set the text syllabically (the setting can be followed in the printed score by following the *Hauptstimme*, the main melodic part, as it crosses between the different instruments), and then removed the words.[15]

An annotated version of the published score – discovered in 1977[16] – in which Berg revealed the previously unknown programme of the work, makes clear not only how extensive this programme was, but also the extent to which it determined details of the formal structures, the pitches, the proportions and even the choice of metronome marks. The four-note cell A-B flat-B natural-F, for example, which acts as the main motivic cell of the work and frequently determines, amongst other things, the choice of row forms and row transpositions, is derived from the initials of Alban Berg and Hanna Fuchs converted into German notation. Similarly, the proportions and the metronome markings of the movements are determined by the two numbers 23 and 10 which Berg regarded as his and Hanna's fateful numbers. In the *Lyric Suite* Berg has, in effect, created an opera libretto (and, as George Perle has observed, has written music that reflects the narrative details

[14] Adorno, Theodor W., *Alban Berg*, trans. Julianne Brand and Christopher Hailey (Cambridge: Cambridge University Press, 1991), p. 104.

[15] There has been some argument about whether Berg ever intended this text to be sung. Since the text follows the instrumental parts – going from the top of the violin register to the bottom of the cello register – the vocal range is obviously impractical as it stands, but there is some evidence that suggests Berg had considered octave transpositions to make it practical. Indeed, there is also, in the sketches, one note at the climax for solo voice undoubled by the instruments. See Perle, George, 'The Secret Programme of the *Lyric Suite*', *Musical Times* 1977, no. 1616, p. 118.

[16] Perle, George, *ibid.*, nos. 1614-1616, pp. 629-32, 709-13, 809-13.

of the libretto in a way that is just as specific as is any of the music of *Wozzeck*), but a libretto that is arranged in such a way as to give a sequence of pure, abstract instrumental musical forms.

The *Lyric Suite* is one of the seminal works of the twentieth century. The textural experiments of the third movement, for example, not only had a direct influence on Bartók but anticipate the music of Penderecki and Lutosławski, while the opening of the last movement explores the relationship between metre, tempo and rhythm in a way that is only comparable to similar explorations in the music of Elliott Carter (see, for example, the penultimate section of Carter's Second Quartet).

Berg published the *Lyric Suite* with a dedication to Zemlinsky, whose *Lyric Symphony* is quoted in the fourth movement of the work. It is fitting, therefore, that Zemlinsky's own final work in the genre, the Fourth Quartet written in 1936, should also be a six-movement suite in memory of Berg who had died the previous year.

*

The rich tradition of the Austro-German quartet came to an end when the National Socialists came to power in January 1933. In April of that year, it was decreed that "civil servants who are not of Aryan descent are to be put into retirement", the term 'civil servants' here including a whole group of employees working in the arts and education such as Schreker, Schoenberg, Bruno Walter, Hermann Scherchen and Jascha Horenstein. By November of that year, the Reichsmusikkammer, which was charged with bringing music into line with National Socialist ideals, had been established.[17]

Some non-Jewish composers, such as Hindemith who was at the centre of an enormous political row that involved both Furtwängler and Goebbels, stayed on for a while. Others, like Schoenberg and Weill, left immediately. Still others, like Zemlinsky, sought refuge in Vienna only to have to move on again in 1938 when Austria was annexed and became a province of the German Reich. Within the space of five years, hundreds of composers, con-

---

[17] Hinton, Stephen, 'Germany 1918-1945' in Morgan, Robert (ed.), *Man and Music: Modern Times*, (London: Macmillan, 1993), p. 101.

ductors, instrumentalists, publishers and musicologists, emigrated to America or to Britain. Hindemith, Krenek, Schoenberg, Wellesz, Weigl and other emigrants continued to write string quartets, the musical language and formal structures of which continued the Austro-German tradition, but these composers were no longer in Germany or even, in most cases, in Europe.

Those composers that remained in Germany and Austria, and who continued to write music of a kind that was not approved by the National Socialists, found their music proscribed. Some, like Karl Amadeus Hartmann (1905-1963), went into a kind of inner exile. Others were less fortunate. Viktor Ullmann (1898-1944), who had been a pupil of Schoenberg and one of the organisers of the Society for Private Musical Performances, was arrested and died in Auschwitz. His last work, *The Emperor of Atlantis*, was written in the concentration camp town of Terezin.

By the time that normal cultural life resumed after the war, musical fashions had changed. The period after the First War had seen a conscious rejection of the artistic philosophy of the pre-war years, in favour of the cultivation of an objective, socially useful art. Now, after the Second World War, there was again a feeling that it was necessary to go back to essentials and the young composers who attended the Darmstadt summer schools in the late '40s and early '50s went about re-examining the whole basis of the musical language. Totally serial pieces, in which every aspect of a work was determined by rigorous serial techniques, became the order of the day and the new language demanded new ensembles and new kinds of forms. It was a language to which the string quartet was thought to have little to contribute. The characteristic German chamber music work of the early 1950s is not a string quartet but a piece like Karlheinz Stockhausen's (b. 1928) *Kreuzspiel* for piano, oboe, bass clarinet and percussion, in which the instrumentation is chosen to make clear the separate and independent serial threads. The nearest Stockhausen has ever got to the string quartet is the so-called *Helikopterquartet*, a work that demands that each performer is in a separate helicopter.

It is perhaps significant that the composer who now seems to embody what is left of both the Austro-German quartet and symphonic tradition should be Hans Werner Henze (b. 1926), a composer who, after an initial involvement with total serialism, deliberately rejected the doctrinaire attitudes and techniques of the

Darmstadt composers and has chosen to live most of his life out-side his native country. Although chamber music has formed only a relatively small part of what, by any reckoning, is an enormous output, Henze's five string quartets are important not only as works in their own right but also because they summarise both his own stylistic development and present, in microcosm, the conflicting artistic pressures facing a composer working in the Austro-German quartet tradition in the second half of the twentieth century. The First Quartet of 1947, a student work written while studying with Fortner, is a formally traditional, neo-Classical piece, the in-fluences on which (primarily those of Stravinsky) are, according to Henze himself, "too obvious to list".[18] The Second Quartet dates from his period of study with René Leibowitz and his first lessons in Schoenbergian serialism (the score even employs Schoenberg's *Haupt-* and *Nebenstimme* indications). All three movements of the work use the same note row – which anyone interested in such things will have no difficulty in tracking down – in a relatively straightforward way.

The last three quartets, conceived as a group of contrasting works, were all written in 1976-7. The Third, a sombre, continu-ously densely-textured, one-movement 'funeral ode' written in memory of Henze's mother, is perhaps the most difficult of the quartets with which to get to grips. The Fourth is the most diverse in that, more than any, it brings together the conflicting stylistic, even notational claims facing composers in the second half of the century. This four-movement piece consists of a largely unmeasured (that is, without bar lines) first movement written in proportional, and occasionally graphic, notation; a second movement that is not only precisely notated (with the exception of some propor-tionally notated cadenzas) but based on a Byrd Pavanne, around the frequently triadic harmonic structure of which the viola weaves an eloquent cantilena; a scherzo movement written in the kind of constantly varying time signatures that appeared in the very first Henze quartet (although without the neo-Classicism of that piece); and a finale for which there is no score, only four separate parts. The parts consist of a series of separate events (precisely notated

[18] Henze, Hans Werner, in the notes to the recording of the complete Henze String Quartets by the Arditti Quartet (WER 60114/15-50)

but often free in dynamics and speed), each contained in its own discrete box. Only the first, central and last events are indicated as such; for the rest the first violin initiates the action and chooses the order in which the events appear ("returning occasionally to the opening theme or parts of it"[19]), while the other players choose from their series of events to react to, or echo, the first violin. The effect – as with the Lutosławski Quartet – is to produce an element of controlled indeterminacy, so that the movement is different at each performance.

The Fifth Quartet, an extraordinarily intense six-movement work, is perhaps the finest of the set. The form, the language and even some of the indications – such as the "*herzschlag* [heartbeat]" marking in the second movement – link the work firmly to the world of the op. 3 Quartet and the *Lyric Suite* of Berg. While the final *Morgenlied* is not, as far as one knows, a 'secret' setting of a text, it is perhaps indicative of Henze's natural affinity to the emotional and compositional world of Berg that he has used this technique elsewhere (in works such as the *Ode to the Western Wind*) and, indeed, arrived at the technique before the discovery of the annotated score of the *Lyric Suite* revealed the method of working Berg employed in the *Largo desolato*. In these last two quartets Henze can be said to anticipate an important aspect of much of the most interesting music of the late twentieth century. The eclecticism of the Fourth and Fifth Quartets – which embrace graphic notation, indeterminacy, serialism, the most straightforward diatonic chords and tonal or even modal progressions – is an attempt to arrive at an all-embracing, non-doctrinaire language that is characteristic of the final years of the twentieth century.

At the time of writing, Henze is in his seventy-sixth year and his last string quartet was written almost a quarter of a century ago. The tradition that initially gave us the genre, and that still forms the backbone of most string quartet concerts, has largely disappeared. The torch has been passed to Russian, Hungarian, French, English, American, Australian and, with Takemitsu, Japanese composers (some of whom will be discussed in the following chapters), in whose hands the genre has found fruitful new areas and directions in which to develop.

---

[19] In the Introduction to the published score of Henze's Fifth Quartet.

II
The French Quartet

Caroline Potter

To my way of thinking, it is quite mad to speak of a 'French tradition'.
Pierre Boulez[1]

A cursory glance at French musical history might suggest that French composers do not favour the string quartet medium. Most French composers were trained at the Paris Conservatoire, an institution which, at least in the nineteenth century and first decades of the twentieth century, favoured vocal music – indeed, the most prestigious prize open to Conservatoire-trained composers, the Prix de Rome, involved the composition of a cantata for three voices, a miniature dramatic work which was viewed as the first step towards a career writing for the opera house. For most of the nineteenth century, opera was considered the most prestigious genre, and if the composition of chamber music was not actively discouraged, the medium certainly suffered from a perceived lack of public appeal compared to opera.

But from 1879, there was a conscious attempt to develop a French tradition of chamber music. In this year, the Société Nationale was founded by a group of French composers as a forum for the promotion of French chamber music. Paradoxically, however, those composers whose string quartets were first performed under the auspices of the Société Nationale in the late nineteenth century (César Franck and many of his pupils, most notably Ernest Chausson and Vincent d'Indy), were those who most submitted to the influence of Wagner. Franck's technique of thematic transformation – derived, of course, from the Wagnerian *leitmotif* – was favoured by many of his followers, and had an impact on Debussy when he composed his only string quartet.

Writing to his friend Chausson, Claude Debussy (1862-1918) confided that he felt fearful when composing the quartet that was to have been dedicated to his correspondent.[2] The Chausson connection is a significant one. Ernest Chausson (1855-1899) was

---

[1] Boulez, Pierre, *Conversations with Célestin Deliège*, (London: Eulenberg, 1976), p. 19.
[2] When Durand published the Quartet in 1894, it was dedicated to the Ysaÿe Quartet.

one of Debussy's closest friends at the time of the composition of the Quartet, though their friendship later cooled, partly, it appears, because Chausson disliked the piece. As a former pupil of Franck, Chausson was both a central figure in the Parisian chamber music scene and an enthusiastic Wagnerite. Like Franck, he employed techniques of thematic transformation in his symphony and various chamber works, techniques which Debussy himself utilised in his Quartet. Evidence from Debussy's letters suggests that the composition of the Quartet was not always an easy process. He restarted the finale three times, perhaps because in the definitive version, the finale gains in momentum, starting with the tempo of the previous slow movement, and this transition proved problematic.

The Quartet was premiered during a Société Nationale concert by the Quatuor Ysaÿe on 29 December 1893. A letter Debussy wrote to Chausson on 5 February the following year reveals his friend's dislike of the work:

> I should also say that I was really upset for several days by what you said about my quartet [...]. Anyway, I'll write another one which will be for you, in all seriousness for you, and I'll try and bring some nobility to my forms.[3]

After Debussy's friendship with Chausson cooled, his plan to write both a second quartet and a violin sonata were abandoned. Not until 1915 did Debussy turn again to Classical forms and abstract titles.

Edvard Grieg's String Quartet in G minor op. 27, composed in 1878, has often been cited as an influence on Debussy's Quartet, despite the fact that Debussy made many less than complimentary remarks about Grieg's music. The two pieces share an overall tonality, and both feature a cyclic theme. In addition to these connections, Debussy's and Grieg's quartets are also linked in their employment of modal inflections within a basically tonal musical language. The links between the movements are more subtly handled in Debussy's Quartet, however, and its string writing is more adventurous, particularly in the scherzo second movement.

[3] Lesure, François and Nichols, Roger (eds.), *Debussy Letters* (London: Faber and Faber, 1987), p. 77.

Debussy's scherzo often has a mechanical character, both in its percussive writing and especially in its use of *ostinati* which are repeated without variation and then discarded. This juxtaposition of material results in a form typical of later works by the composer, and the obsessive repetitions point towards the Stravinsky of the Ballets Russes period. Towards the end of a section based on one or several *ostinati*, Debussy tends to decrease the texture and volume (see, for example, the junction between two sections at bb. 46-55 of the movement), a device which, while clearly articulating sectional divisions, also shows the composer's concern for the spatial dimension of music. It is a device which Berlioz used often in his orchestral and choral works to give the impression of a procession approaching or receding from the listener and which Debussy, another innovator, translates into the smaller chamber music genre. As the influence of an older Russian composer, Alexander Borodin, is evident in the unashamedly Romantic slow third movement, it is perhaps best to consider Debussy's String Quartet as a transitional work in his output.

In the popular imagination, the names of Debussy and Maurice Ravel (1875-1937) are all too often paired, despite the two composers' significant differences in aesthetics and musical language. Nevertheless, there are undeniable similarities between the composers' string quartets. They both wrote only one quartet; both works mention a tonality in the title (though this is less unusual with Ravel); both pieces employ a cyclic theme; and both feature movements that are rhythmically adventurous. Debussy was very enthusiastic about Ravel's Quartet, unlike Fauré, its dedicatee and Ravel's composition teacher at the Conservatoire under whom he was still studying in 1904, the year the Quartet was composed.

Fauré considered the finale of Ravel's Quartet – which is mostly in an unusual 5/8 metre that was probably inspired by Russian folk models – too short. The finale might be in an adventurous metre, but on the whole, like the rest of the Quartet, is somewhat four-square, proceeding by the immediate repetition and diminution of ideas. The only movement to be largely exempt from this criticism is the slow third movement, which seems unable to settle in one tempo. Roger Nichols rightly believes that these constant changes in tempo and texture result in "the continual suppression of the music's natural expression".[4]

The Quartet's first movement starts with a phrase whose symmetrical, rising-then-falling shape seems to epitomise the clichéd view of French music as balanced and poised. It gives no hint of the tension which follows, as almost immediately after this opening, Ravel introduces *tremolandi* and sudden outbursts which contradict the serenity of the opening bars. In the lead up to Figure 10 (the recapitulation), the conflict between tonality and modality, also apparent in Debussy's Quartet, comes to the surface as the cello tries to affirm a cadential figure while the material given to the upper strings hints at the whole-tone mode.

As ever with Ravel, the Quartet is superbly written for the medium and reveals his mastery of instrumental colour. Sometimes, the textures are so dense that they are orchestral in feel. Ravel also evokes the orchestra through imaginative colouristic scoring, an innovation which was to become typical of string quartet writing in the twentieth century. The second movement opens with a variety of string effects; Ravel initially alternates *pizzicato*, bowed and *tremolo* phrases. Some of the percussive rhythmic effects are reminiscent of Ravel's Spanish-inspired works, and the alternation of 6/8 and 3/4 metre at the start of the movement heightens this Hispanic flavour. At Figure 25, Ravel indicates that the second violin should sound like a harp. The third movement also shows that Ravel was searching for unusual sonorities; here, he frequently alternates phrases using *sur la touche* bowing and bowing in the normal position. The second violin is also given an interesting colouristic effect in the finale, at Figure 22. Here, Ravel uses one pitch as a focal note – a device characteristic of him – and this pitch oscillates around different octaves, altering the tone colour for one of its appearances by using a natural harmonic.

French composers of the twentieth century did not tend to approach the string quartet with confidence, and composers as diverse as Olivier Messiaen, Jean Barraqué, Erik Satie and Francis Poulenc avoided the string quartet altogether. It is surely relevant that almost no major French composers have themselves been string players; Milhaud, a violinist, is the only exception who immediately springs to mind. But this probable lack of technical con-

---

[4] Nichols, Roger, *Ravel* (London: Dent, 1977), p. 24.

fidence in the medium is, perhaps, less important than the popular association of the string quartet with the giants of the Austro-German musical world: Haydn, Mozart and Beethoven. French composers' knowledge of the medium's illustrious history and prestige has led them to be daunted by its challenge, and perhaps to feel that it is not part of their cultural baggage. Significantly, Fauré wrote to his wife – a non-musician – on 9 September 1923:

> I have started a quartet for stringed instruments, without piano. This is a genre which Beethoven in particular made famous, and causes all those who are not Beethoven to be terrified of it! [...]. I haven't mentioned it to anyone. I won't say anything about it until I'm approaching the goal, the end of the work.[5]

Fauré (1845-1924), who was unusual amongst French composers of his generation for concentrating on chamber music, finished his only string quartet op. 121 on 11 September 1924, less than two months before his death, noting at the end of the manuscript: "derniers mesures de la dernière œuvre: le quatuor". Similarly, Albert Roussel (1869-1937) only wrote one quartet, his op. 45 (1933-4), and waited until nearly the end of his life to approach the genre which he considered to be "the purest and highest musical form".[6]

Roussel's view that the string quartet is one of the most serious and challenging musical genres was shared by many of his near-contemporaries. Often, a French composer will demonstrate this view by employing a more or less strict contrapuntal form in the quartet. Roussel concluded his four-movement quartet with a fugue, as did Jacques Ibert (1890-1962), a composer not generally associated with serious, abstract music.

The group of composers known as Les Six may have been expected to take a more light-hearted approach to the string quartet. But although the reputation of the group is one of frivolity, they were a very varied group of composers who had only their friendship in common and paid little or no attention to the aes-

---

[5] Jones, John Barrie (ed. and trans.), *Gabriel Fauré: a Life in Letters* (London, Batsford, 1989), p. 202.
[6] Cited in Roy, Jean, 'Les quatuors de Fauré, Debussy, Ravel et Roussel' in *Le quatuor à cordes en France de 1750 à nos jours* (Paris: Association Française pour la Patrimoine Nationale, 1995), p. 130.

thetic stance propounded by Jean Cocteau in his short book *Le coq et l'arlequin* (1918) which was commonly considered to be their artistic manifesto. Cocteau's book praised Satie and popular musical forms, and rejected Wagner and French Wagnerism, (unsurprisingly, given the date of publication). Of the members of the group, only Darius Milhaud, Arthur Honegger and Germaine Tailleferre composed quartets. Honegger (1892-1955) always distanced himself from Cocteau's ideas; his affinity was with Bach and other contrapuntists of the Austro-German tradition. As a student at the Conservatoire, he was perhaps most influenced by André Gédalge, the professor of fugue who believed that the string quartet was "the touchstone for the composer", thus reinforcing the commonly held view of the prestige of the genre. Honegger's two mature quartets were written in 1936 and 1937, but he first approached the genre as early as 1917 in a work in which the density of the contrapuntal writing and extreme chromaticism are more reminiscent of Reger than of any French contemporary; it would be hard to conceive of a work further removed from the aesthetic associated with the soon-to-be-formed Les Six.

Tailleferre's (1892-1983) short three-movement Quartet (which was originally only two movements long and entitled *Sonatine*) was played frequently during the period of Les Six activity (1918-21), being a particular favourite of the all-female Quatuor Morhange. Its unpretentiousness and brevity are certainly a world away from the overblown post-Romanticism despised by Cocteau and his acolytes. As its original title suggests, Tailleferre exhibits the Classical values of restraint and formal clarity in this piece but she also subtly undermines the seriousness which French composers so often associate with the genre and while the first movement is in a relatively straightforward sonata form, the two subsequent movements are more lightweight and based on dance rhythms. She also undermines tonality by incorporating bitonal/modal elements. The first movement, for example, ends on chord V in C sharp minor, leading us to expect a resolution on chord I at the start of the second. However, although the cello outlines this chord in the first bars of the scherzo, the other three instruments contradict this key, being centred on the Phrygian mode on E.

While Tailleferre's Quartet is the only example of this genre in her output – she was a prolific composer – her more industrious fellow member of Les Six, Darius Milhaud (1892-1974) composed eighteen quartets. This quantity is more often associated with eighteenth-century composers, who often published quartets in sets of six, than with those active in the twentieth century, and oddly enough, Milhaud predicted that he would write this number of quartets in *Le Coq*, the short-lived magazine of Les Six. The most notorious of his quartets are surely his fourteenth and fifteenth, known more for their novelty value than for any musical reason, since, ingeniously, they can be played either as separate works or as an octet. While the superimposition of melodies or *ostinati* in different keys was a constant feature of Milhaud's musical style, this possible superimposition of different works is unique.

As Alain Poirier has noted, quartets are particularly thin on the ground in France in the period 1945-60.[7] The mixed chamber work for a flexibly constituted ensemble (of which the London Sinfonietta and the Ensemble Intercontemporain, conceived as a Parisian equivalent of the London ensemble, are typical) has been preferred by French composers, as by those of other nationalities in the twentieth century. Of the most influential composers of the late 1940s and 1950s, Messiaen avoided the quartet genre altogether, while Pierre Boulez (b. 1925) attempted it once, in the *Livre pour quatuor*, but found the result unsatisfactory.

Boulez's view of the status of the string quartet is a traditional one. He wrote in the introduction to a book on the string quartet in the twentieth century that the medium

> requires the composer to devote discipline and care to it; the form brings weaknesses in thought and execution to the surface, it magnifies invention at the same time as it refines it. In short, the string quartet is a test in the sense that it is an initiation.[8]

In conversation with Célestin Deliège, Boulez admitted: "I have what is probably an innate feeling for what one might call the proliferation of basic material",[9] a feeling that is evident not only where an individual work is concerned, but in Boulez's output as a

---

[7] Poirier, Alain, 'Le quatuor à cordes après 1945, entre le genre et le médium instrumental' in *Le quatuor à cordes en France de 1750 à nos jours*, p. 189.
[8] Preface to Goldet, Stéphane, *Quatuors du XXe siècle* (Paris: IRCAM-Papiers, 1987)
[9] Boulez, *op. cit.*, p. 15.

whole: one piece engenders another and, as he admits, "all the works I write are basically different facets of one central work, of one central concept".[10] This Proustian concept of the essential unity of an artist's œuvre is strikingly similar to a remark Dutilleux once made that "an artist has a very small number of things to say which are ever emphasised and ever identical".[11] In the outputs of both Boulez and Dutilleux, there are clear similarities in the details of several works as well as in the overall concept of the work, similarities which go beyond the unity of style one would expect to perceive in the work of a composer with an individual voice. But Boulez has gone further than Dutilleux, by refusing to countenance the notion of the finished work of art. His constant revision of works is the most obvious indication of his penchant for the proliferation of material. Boulez is interested in "forms capable of transformation" (he particularly admires the continuous development in several works by Berg) and as a result, feels that "when it comes to form, German music has influenced me by far the most – and the most German features of German music at that!"[12]

Boulez's *Livre pour quatuor* (1948-9) is a problematic work; even the seemingly straightforward question of the number of movements in the piece is not easy to answer. The composer planned six movements, as follows:

Ia   *Vivo*
Ib   *Moderato*
II   *Assez vif*
IIIa *Assez large*
IIIb *Assez vif, très mobile*
IIIc *Lent, furtif*
IV
V   *Lent, mais mobile*
VI   *Modéré*

Boulez composed only movements I, II, III and V in 1948-9, and added the sixth movement in 1959. The score published by Heugel in 1960 does not feature a fourth movement, and although Boulez

---

[10] *Ibid.*, p. 50.
[11] Quoted in Potter, Caroline, *Henri Dutilleux: His Life and Works* (Aldershot: Ashgate, 1997), p. 59.
[12] Boulez, *op. cit.*, p. 17.

said that it would be "a combination of movements I and II",[13] there is no evidence to suggest that it was ever composed. Moreover, the totality of the composed material of the *Livre* was not performed in public until very recently. The Quatuor Parrenin, which performed the piece several times in the 1950s and '60s, recorded it for the Erato label, but this recording features only movements Ia, Ib, IIIa, IIIb, IIIc and V. The same ensemble gave the British premiere of the complete first and third movements in 1967 but it appears that they never performed the even-numbered movements.

The *Livre* is a pivotal work in Boulez's output, bringing together the contrapuntal density of his first two piano sonatas, a move towards the integral serialism of his next work (*Structures Ia* for two pianos), an element of limited performer choice (because the performers are allowed to select which movements they play) that anticipates the Third Piano Sonata, and the first hint of his intense interest in the aesthetics and poetry of Mallarmé. The title of the quartet already suggests the influence of Mallarmé, although the poet's unfinished *Livre* was not published when Boulez wrote the quartet. In more general terms, the concept of overarching connections between the works of an artist was one Mallarmé often repeated and Boulez found sympathetic. Boulez's Third Piano Sonata, begun in 1957 but never completed was, according to the composer, explicitly inspired by Mallarmé's *Livre*, and it has several features in common with the quartet. For both pieces, Boulez states that the performer may choose to omit certain movements, and for both pieces, he published his plans for the overall structure of the work.

The *Livre pour quatuor* is marked by the influence of Webern and, certainly, the composers of the Second Viennese School are far closer to Boulez than any of his French predecessors in this work. His frequent use of wide intervals, the great variety of modes of playing he employs, and the strong contrast in dynamics, all evoke Webern, though Boulez generally uses denser textures than Webern. The extraordinary fluctuations in tempo perhaps also derive from Webern; Boulez, however, goes far further than the Austrian composer in this respect, and the entire piece, not just

[13] Cited in Jameux, Dominique, *Boulez* (Paris: Fayard, 1984), p. 55.

section IIIb, merits the description 'très mobile'.

Many commentators have considered the *Livre* to be a precursor of Boulez's brief integral serial period. The composer and musicologist André Boucourechliev wrote:

> The obvious taking into hand of all the elements of the musical language by means of a 'generalised series' is imminent [...]. Actually, this taking into hand is being achieved by stealth in the compositional process of the *Livre pour quatuor*. Thus, 'chapter' Ia integrates timbres 'serially', IIIa does the same for durations, and IIIc for volume and attacks ...[14]

In practice, however, it is difficult to see how the *Livre* can be described as an integral serialist work. In movement IIIc, for example, Boulez uses a very wide variety of dynamics and modes of attack, but these do not appear in any fixed order (or any inversion of the order, as far as I can tell). But the movement is interesting, not because of its adherence – or lack of adherence – to a supposed scheme, but because of the clarity of its form (a gradual increase, followed by a corresponding decrease, in dynamic level and in density), and the sheer beauty of its timbral contrasts. In many ways, it heralds Boulez's most recent works (such as *Sur incises* of 1996-8) in the composer's employment of a gesture which moves in time and space from one instrument to another.

There is plenty of evidence to suggest that Boulez became dissatisfied with the quartet soon after it was composed. In 1950, he wrote to John Cage: "Meeting you made me end a 'classical' period with my quartet, which is well behind me now".[15] While Boulez does not elaborate on this, the quartet is the last of his pieces written for relatively traditional genres (his incomplete Third Piano Sonata, for example, is hardly a traditional sonata). Furthermore, problems surfaced during the preparation of a printed score of the work, with Boulez writing to Cage on 30 December 1950 that he was "completely paralysed by copying, on account of that damned quartet", and complaining that he had to copy out two scores,

---

[14] Boucourechliev, André, sleeve note for Erato LP STU 70580 (1969).
[15] Letters of 3, 11, and 12 January 1950; cited in Nattiez, Jean-Jacques (ed.), *The Boulez-Cage Correspondence* (Cambridge: Cambridge University Press, 1993), p. 45.

one with bar-lines for performance – of the parts –, bar-lines that are
in any case no more than a quantification of the values of rhythmic
units between two bar-lines; and on the other hand a score to be
read – a study score – without a single bar-line, but with the real
rhythmic markings, which is to say purely horizontal ones according
to cell.[16]

Moreover, Boulez expressed dissatisfaction with the original scoring of the work because "it posed great interpretative problems for
a quartet, and you would need a conductor to solve them".[17] Realising that the idea of employing a conductor for a string quartet
was absurd, he decided to rework the *Livre pour quatuor* for string
orchestra. This new version, however, was not to be a simple transcription of the quartet version; as he put it:

in an orchestral work one can no longer have the same point of
view, and in the two movements of the *Livre* for string quartet that
became a *Livre* for string orchestra (basically the music is the same),
there is such a degree of proliferation and such an additional weight
of ideas, that it is almost a new piece.[18]

So far, only movements Ia and Ib have been rewritten for string
orchestra, and the revised versions are about sixty per cent longer
than the originals.

Boulez's discontent with the string quartet version of the *Livre*
has, to some extent, been consigned to history. The Alban Berg
Quartet was the first to persuade Boulez that it could be played,[19]
and since 1985, the composer has sanctioned other performances
of the string quartet version. More recently, quartets specialising
in contemporary music, notably the Arditti Quartet, have overcome its technical and interpretive challenges.

*

The question of performer choice also arises in *Archipels II*, the
string quartet by the Bulgarian-born French composer André
Boucourechliev (1925-97). His interest in the concept of the open

---

[16] *Ibid.*, p. 80.
[17] Boulez, *op. cit.*, p. 49.
[18] *Ibid.*
[19] Jameux, *op. cit.*, p. 56.

work stemmed partly from his enthusiasm for Umberto Eco's book *Opera aperta* (1962); indeed, Boucourechliev was the translator of the 1965 French edition of the book. His Quartet, the second of a cycle of five pieces, all of which have the same title ('archipelagos'), features two types of material, the first of which, a continuous thread based on four pitches, may be interrupted by the second. Boucourechliev writes: "[...] an event can be 'called' by one of the performers, whenever he or she wishes, on condition that the others confirm and follow this message."[20] The performers can, therefore, choose one of a very large number of possible navigational routes between the different islands of the archipelago. Francis Bayer contrasts Boucourechliev's use of performer choice with that of Boulez:

> [...] with Boulez, one choice excludes other choices, and consequently there is no true ambiguity; the development of the musical discourse, progressing in one direction and in linear fashion, conforms to the structure of traditional rhetoric. With Boucourechliev, on the other hand, all choices proposed are possible, with none excluding another, resulting in a constant instability, which renders the form of the work variable, its direction multiple and its duration uncertain.[21]

Those composers of the younger generation who did compose string quartets in this post-war period were, in general, those who felt little or no connection with the Austro-German musical tradition. Maurice Ohana (1913-92) wrote three works for string quartet: *Cinq séquences* (1963) and his First and Second Quartets of 1964 and 1980. These works reflect his mixed heritage; a composer of Gibraltarian and Spanish parentage, Ohana was born in Casablanca, was a British passport holder and, for most of his life, a French resident, though he did not take French citizenship until 1976. The influences of African drumming and *cante jondo* (incorporating the microtonal inflections of the flamenco singer) were crucial, as was the example of Debussy's formal freedom and great love of nature. Ohana's interest in stringed instruments focused on their ability to play microtones (he was particularly fond of thirds

---

[20] Boucourechliev [sleeve note], *op. cit.*
[21] Bayer, Francis, *De Schönberg à Cage: essai sur la notion d'espace sonore dans la musique contemporaine* (Paris: Klinksieck, 2 / 1987), p. 168.

of a tone), and on the wide range of colours available from them.

Betsy Jolas (b. 1925), a Paris resident of American origin, has written three quartets to date. The second of these (written in 1966) shows her affinity with the human voice, not least because the first violin is replaced by a *coloratura* soprano. She makes no concessions to the pitching difficulties the vocalist may experience, however, and although the ear is naturally drawn first to the voice, it is treated in the same manner as the instruments in the ensemble. Her employment in this work of space-time notation, where pitch is fixed but duration flexible (though the interaction between the instruments is not left to chance) is characteristic of her style. Space-time notation of this type pre-supposes that all members of the ensemble will be closely attentive to the others – a prerequisite of quartet performances in any age.

*

Ainsi la nuit, which, at the time of writing, forms Henri Dutilleux's (b. 1916) only contribution to the quartet medium (he has spoken of composing a second quartet, possibly with female voice added to the string ensemble[22]), was written between 1973 and 1976 in response to a commission from the Juilliard Quartet (though the Parrenin Quartet gave the first performance on 6 January 1977). This lengthy gestation period (for a work of around seventeen minutes in duration) is characteristic of Dutilleux, a slow and painstaking worker who has written only a dozen or so major works. Not having written for the string quartet since his student days, Dutilleux started the composition process by making a series of technical studies (which do not survive, though fragments of a preliminary version entitled *Nuits* are available for study) and looking closely at other works in the genre, including Beethoven's op. 132 Quartet, Bartók's six quartets and Webern's *Bagatelles*. Significantly, since Dutilleux shares Berg's obsession with symmetry on both the large and small scale, and his commitment to a musical language with some links to tonality, he decided against consulting Berg's *Lyric Suite* as he was afraid of being too heavily

---

[22] In conversation with the author.

influenced by the work.[23] Bartók is probably the strongest influence on *Ainsi la nuit*, not least in Dutilleux's choice of a nocturnal title (which does not refer to any other work of art), and several passages (especially, as one might expect, in the two movements specifically entitled 'Nocturne') are reminiscent of Bartókian 'night music' – evocations of insects, rustling leaves and other natural sounds of a kind that appear in many works by Bartók (in the third movement of the *Concerto for Orchestra*, and in the Fourth and Fifth Quartets, for example). Dutilleux also employs the 'snap' *pizzicato* which is associated with Bartók, and, more generally, the symmetrical overall form of *Ainsi la nuit* is close to the Bartók of the Fifth Quartet.

The work is divided into twelve sections which are played without a break (Dutilleux once wrote that he dislikes breaks between movements as they "spoil music's power to enchant us",[24] and he directs that most of the movements are to *segue*): an introduction, seven movements and four 'parenthesis' sections, arranged as follows:

Introduction (untitled) – *Nocturne* – *Parenthèse I* – *Miroir d'espace* – *Parenthèse II* – *Litanies* – *Parenthèse III* – *Litanies II* – *Parenthèse IV* – *Constellations* – *Nocturne II* – *Temps suspendu*

This demonstrates that the movements entitled 'Litanies' and 'Nocturne' are arranged in symmetrical fashion around the central point of the work. The prime function of the 'parenthesis' sections is to act, in the words of the composer, as reservoirs of material; they anticipate what is to come and recall material which has already been heard, generally in varied, if recognisable, form. The links between different sections are not confined solely to these connections between the parentheses and the named movements, however.[25] This Proustian function of the parentheses, acknowledging the notion that memory is inexact, is an important component of Dutilleux's musical style, and he has on several occasions

---

[23] Nichols, Roger, interview with Dutilleux on 11 April 1991. Part of this interview was published in the *Musical Times* in February 1994 (pp. 87-90); I am grateful to Roger Nichols for providing me with a copy of the complete interview text.

[24] Dutilleux, Henri, preface to the score of his violin concerto, *L'arbre des songes* (Mainz: Schott, 1986).

[25] See Potter *op. cit.*, especially pp. 72-5, for more details about the links between the sections.

referred to the crucial influence of Proust on his music. In addition, each of the parenthesis sections focuses on a particular string technique.

The transformation of musical material can be demonstrated, for example, by comparing the opening bars of the quartet with variants heard at the start of both 'Litanies' and 'Parenthèse IV'. The opening bars and much of 'Litanies' consist of palindromic figurations, a musical device favoured by Bartók and Berg as well as Dutilleux. This symbolic return to the point of origin again exhibits Dutilleux's preoccupation with the interlinked notions of time and memory. The second named movement, 'Miroir d'espace', is a mirror in several spatial dimensions: the movement is, again, palindromic (excluding a brief passage at the centre), and the strikingly high first violin line is literally reflected by the cello at a distance of six octaves or more, with the cello entering a quaver behind the first violin, to ensure that both lines are audible.

Although Dutilleux's interest in the transformation, rather than straightforward repetition, of musical material could be paralleled with Franck's employment of cyclic form, Dutilleux does not welcome these comparisons. Rather than dwell on Franck's often crude attempts to link the four movements of his quartet by, for example, stating the themes one by one prior to their assimilation in the finale, Dutilleux would, I am sure, prefer to highlight the influences of Proust on his concept of musical time, and Debussy's String Quartet on his methods of thematic transformation. But whatever Dutilleux's reservations about being spoken of in the same breath as Franck and his school, it is clear that his use of thematic transformation has a distinguished history in French string quartet writing.

Of the younger generation of composers, Pascal Dusapin (b. 1955) is the composer of two of the most impressive recent French quartets: his Second (*Time Zone*, 1988-90) and Third (1992) Quartets (he wrote a short first quartet in 1982-3 when he was in residence at the Villa Medici in Rome). Richard Toop has written that, when he composed *Time Zone*, Dusapin conceived the notion of the 'infinite quartet', where "each new work in a potentially infinite series [...] would be a commentary on its predecessor and, perhaps, a dream of the problems to be faced by its successor".[26]

---

[26] *Ibid.*

This interrelationship of different works by one composer again evokes the ideas of Boulez and Dutilleux. Dusapin himself has written: "Only the string quartet is suited to music whose lines, interrelationships and flow of musical energy concentrate on the mechanics of the music and the complexity of its relationships."[27]

Although Dusapin's view of the genre would, therefore, appear to be a traditional one, *Time Zone* suggests that his approach to the medium is anything but conventional. The quartet is divided into twenty-four 'zones', although twelve of these play continuously. If these numbers suggest a serial approach to musical language, or perhaps a reference to the twenty-four hours of the day, Dusapin insists that the title of the piece is simply a metaphor, and a reference to the fact that the quartet was written in many different cities (Tokyo, Rotterdam, New York, Brussels, Geneva and Paris). The four string instruments are often treated as soloists or as members of sub-ensembles within the quartet. The first zone starts with a solo instrument, and the four instruments only appear as an ensemble at the end of this movement. Zone Eight is an aggressive violin solo, enigmatically concluding with the inscription "Beckett est mort…". The thirteenth zone features a single line fragmented between the four instruments, and for most of the fifteenth and sixteenth zones, the instruments play in unison. The work is a quartet only in the sense that it is written for the traditional string quartet ensemble; like Elliott Carter, Dusapin rejects the expectation that the four instruments will work together in the traditional way.

Dusapin's Second and Third Quartets have been recorded by the Arditti Quartet, who have commissioned works from many contemporary French composers. The continued existence of distinguished ensembles, together with the quality and quantity of the string quartet repertoire, will surely guarantee the survival of the string quartet medium well into the twenty-first century.

[27] Cited in the sleeve note of the Arditti Quartet recording of his Second and Third Quartets (Audivis-Montaigne MO782016).

III
The Central European Quartet

Amanda Bayley

If there is a common thread linking the variety of string quartet writing by composers of the Central European countries in the early twentieth century then it is the influence of folk music. This played an important part in extending tonal language and in helping composers to retain an identity with their native countries during a time of political turmoil, wherever in the world they happen to have settled. The modalities associated with 'national' styles have helped to replace traditional tonality and for some composers textural and timbral qualities have become important structural features of the music.

In order to shape the content of this chapter, composers have generally been grouped according to their nationality: Hungary (Kodály and Bartók), Romania (Enescu), Czechoslovakia (Martinů, Hába), Poland (Szymanowski, Bacewicz, Penderecki, Lutosławski). The exceptions are Ligeti and Kurtág – two living Hungarian composers who are dealt with at the end of the chapter – and Leoš Janáček (1854-1928). Although Janáček did not write his two quartets until the 1920s, when folk music had already made an impact on the quartets of Zoltán Kodály (1882-1967) and Béla Bartók (1881-1945), he was the first composer to have undertaken extensive folksong research.

A spirit of nationalism preoccupied Janáček to the extent that Czechoslovakian folksong and speech inflection became the fundamentals of his musical thinking from the time he began to collect folksongs in 1885. Like Bartók and Kodály some twenty years later, he aimed to reproduce these songs and their manner of performance. His quasi-scientific research involved the classification of melodies as well as observations of the people who sang them, their dialects and songs, their instruments and dances. He was most interested in the folk music traditions of Eastern Moravia because of the rich melody and rhythmic irregularities they shared with word-based Slovak, Hungarian and Romanian folk music, compared with the more four-square shapes of Bohemian and West Moravian folk musics and the regular dance rhythms of instrumentally-based German and Austrian folk music.

For Janáček the most natural genres for exploring the linguistic properties of folk music were the operas which form the bulk of his output. However, he also absorbed the melodic and rhythmic elements of human speech into his instrumental works, transferring the realism of his operas to an instrumental idiom largely through his treatment of the motif as "an intimate connection between life and art".[1] Janáček was equally fascinated by the Russian realists of the nineteenth century and, in the First Quartet (1923), specifically by Leo Tolstoy's novel, *The Kreutzer Sonata*. The Second Quartet (1928) is autobiographical rather than programmatic. It is directly related to a series of 'Intimate Letters' written to Kamila Štösslová during the composer's old age, following their long companionship. The work follows the progress of a spiritual relationship from first meeting to the end. Significantly, Janáček originally intended the viola part to be played on the viola d'amore.

Like many of Janáček's works, both string quartets are built from short, often self-contained sections reminiscent of the repetitive nature of folksongs and dances. Although there are sonata-form characteristics, Janáček's compositional technique more readily adapts to the notion of repetition, variation and contrast than to any progressive thematic development. He makes much use of held notes related to the drone of bagpipes accompanying a folk melody. (Bartók similarly uses drones in the opening of the Third Quartet (1927) and in the third movement of his Fourth Quartet (1928)). Both of Janáček's quartets have four movements and both begin with short melodies which act as motto themes throughout. Different moods are created by changes to tempo markings, rhythmic changes in accompanying figures, and specific timbral effects: *tremolando, sul ponticello* and trills are used to create effects as well as to serve transitional ends.

Janáček's attitude to the use of folksong parallels Bartók's and although he initially used authentic melodies, he subsequently came to believe that "folk songs should be studied but then used only as models. One should compose original music *in the spirit* of the models".[2] This spirit of East Moravian folk music is expressed in

[1] This point has been convincingly argued by Skoumal, Zdeněk Denny, in 'Structure in the Late Instrumental Music of Leoš Janáček', Ph.D. dissertation, City University, New York (1993), pp. 62-71.
[2] Quoted by Skoumal, Zdeněk Denny, in *op. cit.*, p. 20.

the First Quartet in terms of modal intervals – specifically the Lydian (augmented) fourth, often found in Janáček's music. He explained his modal style, saying that melodies without leading notes keep the tonality fluid and that the expressive power of a melody is enhanced when the emphatic step from leading note to tonic is omitted.[3] The harmonic writing in both quartets is heavily influenced by modal progressions and by the frequent juxtaposition of 'unrelated' harmonies and tonal regions.

Unlike the First Quartet, which refers to East Moravian folk music, the Second reduces the folk element to a 'gypsy scale' defined by the augmented seconds between the third and fourth notes and usually between the sixth and seventh, although here Janáček has flattened the B (see Examples 1a and 1b).

Ex. 1a Janáček, String Quartet no. 2, bb. 9-14

Ex. 1b The gypsy scale

Despite the lack of key signatures in the Second Quartet Janáček never completely abandons a tonal framework. There are perhaps more frequent and more chromatic harmonic contrasts than in the First Quartet, with the development of the main thematic material being more characteristic of late Romantic compositions, but as far as he was concerned "there is no music without key. Atonality abolishes definite key, and thus tonal modulation [...]

[3] Hollander, Hans, Leoš Janáček. His Life and Work, trans. Paul Hamburger (London: John Calder, 1963), p. 95.

Folk song knows of no atonality…".[4] This was a view that Bartók also expressed and which was no doubt felt by other twentieth-century 'nationalist' composers.[5]

Bartók's contribution to the twentieth-century string quartet is characteristically innovative as is his contribution to other genres. Indeed, Bartók's experiences of folk music subsequently inspired him, in the 1920s, to experiment with instrumental techniques previously unheard of in the string quartet repertoire. His near contemporary, Zoltán Kodály, could in some ways be considered less progressive. Bartók's harmonic techniques achieve a new tonal synthesis whereas Kodály's technique is more traditional, his approach to tonality more reticent, using modes as a way of colouring an underlying diatonic harmony. As students of the Budapest Academy of Music, they were each taught by János Koessler. Their interests later converged on the area of folk music, initially as a political reaction to the predominance of German language and culture in Budapest and in support of the Independence Movement (following the Hungarian War of Independence, 1948-49). As a result of this movement, the Hungarian Millennium was being celebrated at the turn of the century which brought with it an upturn in nationalism. This political context provided a background for Bartók and Kodály to begin collecting, and later transcribing, Hungarian folksongs. Their co-ordinated field trips from 1905 benefited from Kodály's experience as the author of a thesis *A Magyar népdal strófaszerkezete* [*The Stanzaic Structure of Hungarian Folk Song*] (Ph.D., Pazmány Péter University, 1906) and this was followed by their joint publication of *Hungarian Folksongs* for voice and piano in 1906. Bartók, however, felt that in order to learn more about Hungarian folk music he needed to gain familiarity with the musical traditions of neighbouring Slovakians, Romanians and South Slavic people. His collecting trips therefore took him further afield which added an extra richness to the influences of folk music in his own works.

Describing Kodály as "one of the most outstanding composers

---

[4] *Ibid.*, p. 119.
[5] 'Folk music of atonality is completely inconceivable' Bartók wrote in his 1931 essay 'On the significance of folk music'. Suchoff, Benjamin (ed.), *Béla Bartók Essays* (London: Faber and Faber, 1976; repr. Lincoln, Nebr., and London: University of Nebraska Press, 1992), p. 345.

of our day" in 1921, Bartók holds him as an exemplar of how "the ancient music of the Hungarian peasants, the only existing musical tradition, [can] serve as a basis for the creation of a new Hungarian music".[6] For Bartók, Kodály's music encapsulated the fundamental ethos of *Magyarság* [Hungarianness].

The two quartets by Kodály, op. 2 (1909) and op. 10 (1918) and the first two by Bartók, op. 7 (1909) and op. 17 (1917), represent their early compositional styles. All four works were premiered in Budapest soon after they were written and share both a Classical and a folk heritage to varying degrees. But while Kodály's First Quartet retains a traditional four-movement design, Bartók's is in three movements. The melodic material of both composers is evidently influenced by Hungarian folksong, while their harmonic language trades on a more recent discovery of the music of Debussy. Kodály's contains much imitative writing and has a strong tonal basis despite its alternation between pitch centres a tritone apart.

Kodály's Second Quartet is in two movements although the second begins with a lengthy, slow introduction that makes it feel like a separate slow movement. Its typically folkish repetitions might suggest any one of the numerous folksongs collected during this period. Kodály here selects six themes all of clearly different folkish character. But, to paraphrase Bartók (who shares Janáček's philosophy), it is only when neither peasant melodies nor imitations of peasant melodies can be found in a composer's music that we may observe him to have completely absorbed the idiom of peasant music which has become his musical mother tongue.[7]

In describing Kodály's music generally, Bartók identifies the following characteristics:

> a melodic force which is amply spread, an absolute knowledge of form, and a certain tendency toward melancholy and excitement [...] Kodály's music does not belong to the kind of music called *modern*: it has no relation whatever to the new atonal and polytonal schools and is still based on the principle of tonal equilibrium. But his language is new, expressing something hitherto untold and demonstrating that tonality has not yet lost its reason for existence.[8]

---

[6] 'On Modern Music in Hungary', (1921) in *ibid.*, pp. 477-478.
[7] 'The Influence of Peasant Music on Modern Music' (1931), in *ibid.*, p. 344.
[8] 'On Modern Music in Hungary', (1921) in *ibid.*, p. 478.

Following its premiere, Kodály's Second, and last, Quartet was widely performed across Europe and in the Soviet Union. Of all the composers who wrote string quartets in the twentieth century, Bartók is among the best known, often rated alongside Beethoven for his lifelong development of the genre. Many composers in the second half of the century considered Bartók's string quartets to be pivotal and therefore used him as a yardstick to measure their own developments against or, indeed, to progress beyond, extending the repertoire of instrumental techniques even further. His six quartets span almost his entire compositional career from 1909 to 1939 continuing the Austro-German tradition in terms of their motivic concision and thematic transformation.

His First Quartet is still under the shadow of late Romantic German music together with that of Debussy, as shown in the simple rondo form of the first movement. This work is closely related to the posthumously published First Violin Concerto that Bartók wrote for the young violinist Stefi Geyer in 1908, the year before the Quartet's completion. Bartók himself revealed the connection between the first four notes of the Quartet and the second movement of the Violin Concerto, which he referred to as his funeral dirge following his unrequited love.[9] The chromaticism and frequent modulations in the Quartet obscure any stable, long-term tonal references. Nevertheless, thematic unity is achieved between movements: the subsidiary function of semitones in the first movement becomes a primary motivic constituent of the *Allegretto* second and *Allegro vivace* third, the latter also featuring the falling sixth of the Geyer motif. Evidence of Bartók's early folk music researches is especially noticeable in the expressive *parlando rubato* melody heard at the outset of the finale, and in the accented short-long rhythm of the Hungarian *verbunkos* introduced later.

The Second Quartet (1917) already demonstrates a richer harmonic vocabulary and a more comprehensive synthesis of folk music than the First. The composer's own writings show how his folk music research fuelled his imagination with new ways of building chords, especially using intervals of fourths, augmented fourths

---

[9] See Dille, Denijs, 'Angaben zum Violinkonzert 1907, den *Deux Portraits*, dem Quartett op. 7 und den Zwei rumänischen Tänzen', *Documenta Bartókiana* 2 (1965), p. 92.

(tritones) and wholetones.[10] These same intervals feature throughout the work's three movements as does the conflict between major and minor thirds drawn from folk sources and explored both harmonically and melodically. The sense of a tonal centre overall is achieved through pitch repetition rather than as a result of traditional chord progressions. While the outer movements are loosely based on sonata form, the central *Allegro* is in rondo form and has an Arabic 'twang' suggestive of Bartók's travels in the Biskra region in 1913.[11]

Bartók's Third Quartet (1927) marks the beginning of his intensely Expressionist style already hinted at during the atonal tendencies of the third movement of the Second Quartet. The work begins with a cluster chord (C sharp-D-D sharp-E) heard as an accompanying drone to the main motivic ideas. This chord at first appears to conceal any firm pitch centricity but it in fact contains, in embryo, the tonal centres for each ensuing section of the work. The form of the work follows the scheme of a one-movement sonata consisting of a *Prima parte, Seconda parte, Ricapitulazione della prima parte* and *Coda*. C sharp is the main tonal reference in the *Prima parte* while a semitonal shift makes D and E flat the competing tonalities in the *Seconda parte*.

This formal concentration encompasses the micro- as well as the macro-structure with melodic, harmonic and rhythmic contrasts being more purposefully and economically consolidated than in any other of his quartets. His variation technique shows how themes are the outcome of an ongoing development, penultimately revealing that the *Ricapitulazione della prima parte* is less a literal recapitulation than a condensed redefinition of earlier motivic and thematic statements. Textural and articulative developments are a novel aspect of Bartók's Third Quartet that he was to pursue in subsequent works and that were to take on an all-important character-defining role in the quartets of later twentieth-century composers.

Although Bartók was, of course, aware of Western European developments, as far as he was concerned, writing in 1920, "the time to establish a system in our atonal music is not at all here as

---

[10] 'The Folk Songs of Hungary' (1928) in Suchoff (ed.), *op. cit.*, p. 338. See also 'Harvard Lectures' (1943), pp. 369-370.
[11] See Kárpáti, János, 'Early String Quartets' in Gillies, Malcolm (ed.), *The Bartók Companion* (London: Faber and Faber, 1993), p. 238.

yet".[12] The furthest he ever travelled towards a systematic atonality was in the Fourth Quartet (1928), where all twelve notes are contained within the first two-bar phrase. However, their organisation soon identifies the parameters of interval and rhythm as being more important than pitch in motivic development. Bartók's repertoire of transformational techniques is here taken to extremes, extending the original motif (b. 7), developing it through inversion, imitation, fragmentation, rhythmic variation and diatonic expansion. The arch form of the whole links first and fifth, second and fourth movements and includes the first instance of the 'snap' *pizzicato* for which Bartók is widely known (whereby the string is plucked between two fingers to rebound on the fingerboard) – a direct reference to folk music.

Folk influences are evident throughout Bartók's quartets but the most explicit and most advanced are in the Fourth where they seem to have been uppermost in his mind. The last movement has an Arab-like theme set against a percussive accompaniment with accents irregularly grouped in twos and threes, indicative of Bulgarian music.[13] In the third movement Bartók explores the changing timbre of non-*vibrato* and *vibrato* to colour the bagpipe-like drone of the chord that accompanies the *parlando rubato* melody in the form of an 'old'-style Hungarian folksong.

The Fifth Quartet (1934) follows an arch form not unlike that of the Fourth but with the alternation of fast and slow movements reversed. Between these movements Bartók continually varies his initial melodic fragments in different contexts identified by accompanying *ostinati*, repeated-note rhythms and punctuating cluster chords, all familiar from previous quartets. The rhythmic momentum is the most striking feature of this piece and in the central scherzo characteristically asymmetrical rhythms evoke folk music from Bulgaria.

The Sixth Quartet (1939) is designed as a cyclic form where the opening ritornello *Mesto* theme recurs at the beginning of the first three movements and finally grows into the closing movement. This form allows Bartók to maintain unifying thematic rela-

[12] 'The Problem of the New Music' (1920) in Suchoff (ed.), *op. cit.*, p. 338. See also 'Harvard Lectures' (1943), p. 457.
[13] See Kárpáti, János, *Bartók's Chamber Music*, trans. Fred MacNicol and Mária Steiner, trans. rev. Paul Merrick (New York: Pendragon Press, 1994), pp. 101-105.

tionships by connecting each of the movements to certain elements of the ritornello itself. In the folk context of the 'bear-dance theme' of the *Burletta* third movement, quarter-tone clashes between the *glissandi* violins recreate the authentically, 'mistuned' effect of folk music performance. Bartók's interest in micro-intervals stemmed from his folksong transcriptions where he invented a system to differentiate intervals of approximately a quarter-tone (marked ♯/2, ♭/2) and less than a quarter-tone by using upward or downward arrows above the note.[14] In 1944 he introduced microtonality on a wider scale as it affects the concept of form in the last movement of the Sonata for Solo Violin. (In the original version he used quarter-tones as a structural principle which were deleted in an edition published by Yehudi Menuhin.[15])

The Romanian, George Enescu (1881-1955), is perhaps even now more famous as a violinist, conductor, even a teacher of the young Menuhin, than as a composer, which makes his position in this chapter somewhat unique. Menuhin's recollection of his teacher's extraordinary musical memory helps to explain how Enescu was able to find time to compose as well as to fulfil the commitments of a busy concert diary:

> Ravel burst in with the manuscript of his newly completed Violin Sonata, and asked Enescu to play it with him that evening for the publishers. [...] they read the work through, Enescu stopping occasionally to ask for clarifications. Then they resolved to play it through once more – and Enescu closed his part and played the entire Sonata from memory.[16]

Enescu began writing his First Quartet op. 22, in 1916, continued it in 1918, and completed it in 1920; the Second was to follow thirty-one years later – one of the last pieces he wrote. Each has four movements, reflecting his tendency to follow traditional structures. However, being some forty-six minutes long, the First Quartet requires repeated hearings to gain a sense of orientation

---

[14] See Somfai, László (ed.), *Hungarian Folk Music Gramophone Records with Béla Bartók's Transcriptions* (Budapest: Hungaroton, 1981), LPX 18058-60.

[15] Peter Bartók has since published an Urtext edition (London: Boosey & Hawkes, 1994).

[16] Malcolm, Noel, *George Enescu: His Life and Music* (London: Toccata Press, 1990), pp. 177-178.

and familiarity, especially as no full score is available, only individual parts. His musical language is strongly Romantic in character and more obviously tonally based than any other Central European composer discussed so far. The third movement of the First
Quartet is perhaps the most interesting in terms of its use of folk
music and as the scholar Noel Malcolm has pointed out "the harsh
and resonant use of folk elements comes at times curiously close
to Janáček".[17] In an interview in 1924 Enescu remarked that "the
only thing one can do properly with folk music [is] to 'rhapsodise
it, with repetitions and juxtapositions' " and later in 1928 said,
"You can develop a folk tune in only one way: dynamic progres-
sion and repetition". As far as he was concerned "an essential feature of folk song is the way it distances itself from harmony: the
lightest harmonising is the most authentic".[18] Through these procedures he retained a Romanian spirit and melodic colouring,
moulding these to his individual processes of melodic and harmonic development, much as with Bartók's use of Hungarian material. This apart, the sound world of the two composers could
scarcely be more different.

The prolific Czech composer, Bohuslav Martinů (1890-1959),
a colleague of Enescu in New York, is widely regarded as being
second only to Janáček in importance among Czechs, even though
he lived in Paris from 1923 until the outbreak of war and thereafter in the USA. Unlike his compatriot, Martinů composed in a
wide variety of instrumental and vocal genres. Yet compared with
the dramatic and literary characters that permeate all Janáček's
works, Martinů draws sharp distinctions between the different genres in which he writes.

Juvenilia apart, Martinů's seven string quartets span almost thirty
years from 1918-1947. The quartet composed in 1918, now known
as no. 1, shows signs of Smetana on the one hand, and Bruckner,
Richard Strauss and Mahler on the other. Martinů himself defined
this four-movement work as belonging to his Impressionist period.
Nonetheless, its first and last movements just as strongly recall the
sound world of Dvořák.

The remaining six quartets date from his maturity. The Second

[17] Ibid., p. 137.
[18] These quotes are all taken from Malcolm, Noel, ibid., pp. 65-66.

(1925) was the first composition to bring international acclaim, being unanimously praised at its first performance in Berlin in 1925. There is evidence of a tonal structure both between and within its three movements although extended chromatic passages contrast with the fundamentally tonal thematic material. Some of his more adventurous harmonies hint at a temporary polytonal conception. The Third Quartet (1929) demonstrates a 'new' and more modern rhythmic and harmonic complexity which the composer has described as having a brittle chamber music texture "as if made of china".[19] Set within a non-tonal background without key signatures, the joyous, lively character of the outer movements have a sustained rhythmic energy that frames the restfully dissonant slow movement. Trills, *tremolando*, harmonics, *sul ponticello* and *col legno* sound effects abound.

During the 1930s, Martinů worked with Bohemian and Moravian folk texts and melodies and some of these folk melodies reappear in the context of more dissonant harmonies in the Fourth Quartet (1937). His characteristically thick, often crowded, string textures are especially prominent in this work, allowing little time for contemplation or reflection. The explosive rhythmic interest in the Fifth Quartet (1938) overshadows the effect of other parameters and shows that the dance rhythms of his native land are always present.

Following the outbreak of the Second World War, Martinů moved to the United States where he wrote his two last quartets, each of which harks back to earlier forms in its three-movement construction. While the Sixth (1946) explores ever more animated textures and displays infinite rhythmic variety, the Seventh, *Concerto da camera* (1947), is more conventional. Though its title is neo-Classical (as are those of several other works) it is only the delicacy of some of the textures that rekindles a neo-Classical spirit. However, there is a more obvious tonal orientation than in the previous four quartets and Martinů is more reserved in his textural and timbral exploits.

Alois Hába (1893-1973), a much more radical yet still largely unknown Czech composer, was the first to experiment with

---

[19] Šafránek, Miloš, *Bohuslav Martinů: His Life and Works*, trans. Roberta Finlayson-Samsourová (London: Allan Wingate, 1962), p. 126.

microtonality on a large scale, writing harmonic-polyphonic works in quarter-tone, fifth-tone and sixth-tone systems. He wrote sixteen string quartets between 1919 and 1967 of which six are written in quarter-tone, two in fifth-tone and three in sixth-tone systems. The theoretical foundations of his microtonal system are to be found in his books and articles published mostly in Czech and some in German.[20] As a violinist himself, Hába wrote his first microtonal pieces for string instruments (the earliest being the Suite for string orchestra, 1917) on which the music could be performed without great technical difficulty, but he soon extended the compositional technique to include choruses, music for wind and for brass instruments, piano pieces and opera. Following initial composition lessons with Vítězslav Novák in Prague (1914-15) he studied with Franz Schreker at the Academy of Music in Vienna (1918-20) then at the College of Music in Berlin (1920-23). While in Berlin, Hába made plans for quarter-tone instruments which were constructed after his return to Prague where he established a department of microtonal music at the Conservatoire.

The idea for developing microtonal music stemmed from his early acquaintance with the folksongs from his native region, Eastern Moravia (Wallachia): his mother, an experienced folk singer, taught Hába local peasant songs which he later studied more closely. In these he heard intervals that deviated from the semitone system and noticed that the soloists would spontaneously modify the pitch of the notes they were singing in order to enhance its expression. He adapted these expressive qualities, stressing the major mode with quarter-tone and sixth-tone sharps and the minor mode with quarter-tone flats. In the Preface to the score of the Second Quartet op. 7 (1920) – the first quartet to use quarter-tones – he wrote: "It is my concern to permeate the semitone system with more delicate sound nuances, not to abolish it [...] to extend the possibilities of expression already given by the old sys-

---

[20] *Harmonické základy čtvrttónové soustavy* [*Harmonic Rudiments of the Quarter-tone System*] (Prague: Hudební matice Umělecké besedy, 1922). *O psychologii tvoření, pohybové zákonitosti tónové a základech nového hudebního slohu* [*On the Psychology of Formation, the Motion Laws of Tones, and the Foundations of Modern Musical Style*] (Prague: Hudební matice Umělecké besedy, 1925), (Vienna: Universal Edition, 1925). *Neue Harmonielehre des diatonischen, chromatischen 1/4-, 1/3-, 1/6-, und 1/12-Tonsystems* (Leipzig: Kistner und Siegel, 1927).

tem".[21] In order to represent this new pitch notation on the page, Hába modified the accepted accidentals (sharps, flats, naturals) as shown in Example 2.

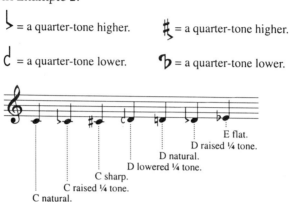

$\flat$ = a quarter-tone higher.　　$\sharp$ = a quarter-tone higher.

$\flat$ = a quarter-tone lower.　　$\flat$ = a quarter-tone lower.

E flat.
D raised ¼ tone.
D natural.
D lowered ¼ tone.
C sharp.
C raised ¼ tone.
C natural.

Ex. 2 Hába's modification of accidentals

With this new pitch language Hába still retained a formal structure of four connected sections – *Allegro non troppo, Scherzando, Largo, Allegro agitato* – in the Second Quartet, as well as imitative, contrapuntal techniques that he had inherited. However, only two years later, in the Third Quartet op. 12 (1922), and in subsequent works, he was composing in a so-called non-thematic style where no musical idea is repeated even on a large scale. Bartók's reaction to this procedure was that it

> abolishes the basic law according to which graspable structure or form can be created only by repeats of various kinds. No structure whatever is imaginable in music, if no repeats are used. In other words, Hába's elimination of structure from musical works is a rather barren conception of music.[22]

The extent to which Hába succeeded in either of his revolutionary aims may well be questioned. An initial response is that much of it sounds out of tune. An all-encompassing use of microtonality, where quarter-tones affect a large proportion of the

---

[21] Sadie, Stanley (ed.), *The New Grove Dictionary of Music and Musicians* (London: Macmillan, 2001), Vol. 10, p. 631.
[22] Suchoff (ed.), 'Harvard Lectures' (1943), *op. cit.*, p. 356.

notes all the way through a piece, brings into question its expressive purpose and confirms Bartók's accusation of 'overcomplication':

> when neighbouring quarter tones are used simultaneously, in the form of double stops, rather disagreeable by-products of sound appear: pulsating beats similar to those produced on the piano when one or two of the strings which serve a key is slightly off pitch. The continuous presence of these unintended pulsations makes polyphonic quarter tone music almost unbearable.[23]

Later on, however, Hába's quarter-tones adopt a pedagogic role (for example in the Sixteenth Quartet, 1967), thus more convincingly enhancing their expressive qualities. But this still does not meet Bartók's reservation that "there is no solution: laws and phenomena of physics cannot be annihilated by any kind of revolution".[24]

Few composers have continued in this vein. Experiments in microtonality have largely been sporadic, mainly connected with electronic music. Hába successfully drew attention to aspects of music not considered mainstream, yet he himself remains a curiosity: it is not even possible to obtain scores or recordings of all his music.

By contrast, although Karol Szymanowski (1882-1937) wrote only two string quartets his contribution to the history of Polish music cannot be overestimated. The revolution in Polish music at the beginning of the twentieth century took place chiefly in Szymanowski's works and, as a consequence, he was a model for the following generation of composers. His studies necessitated thorough familiarity with the achievements of, and new developments in, Western music. However, the surrounding cultural environment in Poland did not encourage progressive trends in Polish music. So in 1901, along with several other composers, Szymanowski acted to form the group 'Young Poland in Music'. This group had parallels with the literary movement 'Young Poland' and adopted Stanisław Przybyszewski's extreme doctrine "Art has no aim, it is aim in itself… Art stands above life, penetrates the essence of the universe […] It becomes its priest."[25] The aims and philosophy of this group are purported to have had "considerable

[24] *Ibid.*, pp. 355-356.
[24] *Ibid.*
[25] Sadie, Stanley (ed.), *op. cit.*, Vol. 24, p. 894.

bearing on the underlying impulses which shaped [Szymanowski's] musical language, particularly in the works composed before 1920".[26]

From 1914 Szymanowski's increasing interest in Russian and French music helped to dispel the German influences which had so depressed composers around this period, while stimulating a prolific creative period during the war years. The First Quartet op. 37 (1917), returns to the sonata structures of his early 'Viennese' compositions, and with it, clearly defined tonal references, especially in the first two movements. The piece was originally designed to have four movements but the projected finale, a fugue, was never written. Instead, the second and third movements were reversed, turning the *scherzando alla burlesca* into a finale. This movement turned out to be an interesting experiment in polytonality, each instrument having a different key signature. Ten years later, the Second Quartet op. 56, also in three movements, has no key signatures at all and allows a freer conception of sonata structure.

In the period between the two quartets, Szymanowski, like the Czech and Hungarian composers, was similarly drawn to the exotic culture of his own country. Folk music from the Tatra highlands strongly influenced the Mazurkas op. 50 (1924-26) – a twentieth-century response to Chopin – and the first act of the ballet *Harnasie* (not completed until 1931). In the slow finale of the Second Quartet an authentic folk melody is chosen for the fugue subject. The *scherzando* second movement has *fortissimo* chords in unison rhythms based on repeated-note motifs, interspersed with canonic writing, which are characteristic of Bartók's Third Quartet, also written in 1927. Again like Bartók, Szymanowski expresses *portamento* in the form of imitative *glissandi*, at Figure 13 in the score. There are further parallels between the two composers' textures but those of Szymanowski lack the rhythmic complexity and harmonic richness of Bartók's.

Like Janáček, Szymanowski relies on rapidly changing moods, achieved through dynamic extremes as well as changes in tempo, texture and timbre. He also experiments with specific string sonorities such as *sul tasto*, *sul ponticello*, *tremolando* and harmonics

---

[26] Samson, Jim, *Music in Transition: A Study of Tonal Expansion and Atonality, 1900-1920* (London: Dent, 1977), p. 130.

in order to differentiate sections of the music, the only specifically defined tonality occurring at the end of movements. As a consequence of this lack of harmonic goal direction, some of Szymanowski's static structures, such as the oscillating *tremolando* opening to the Second Quartet, suggest a more 'impressionist' style reminiscent of Ravel.

Szymanowski encouraged his successors to seek more modern French and Russian styles rather than to imitate his own music. Most young Polish composers therefore went to study abroad, mainly in Paris with Nadia Boulanger who played an important role in shaping the direction of their music. In this they were much influenced by the neo-Classical aesthetic of Stravinsky, Prokofiev, Milhaud and Poulenc. One of these young Polish composers who contributed considerably to the country's musical heritage and bridged the gap between the neo-Romanticism of Szymanowski and the modernism of Lutosławski was Grażyna Bacewicz (1909-1969), once described by an English critic as "the first lady of music".[27] Another violinist/composer, her studies in Paris helped to expand her compositional skills and her first stylistic period, representing her development of neo-Classical forms, includes the first two string quartets (1938 and 1943).

Immediately following the Second World War, both political and social conditions had a strong impact on creativity. The Nazi occupation of Poland inevitably gave composers the urge to express their anti-German emotional responses in their music. The second period of Bacewicz's works, which include the Third (1947), Fourth (1951) and Fifth (1955) Quartets, thus reflects the neo-Expressionism of the early post-war years in combination with a neo-Classical counterpoint and a folk music style. For the Fourth Quartet she received first prize at the International Composers' Competition in Liège and later received awards for other compositions.

Bacewicz objected to the categorisation of her works as neo-Classical yet, as for many other composers, her adherence to this basic style can be attributed to the cultural and political climate at the time. Unlike earlier composers from Central Europe her use of folk materials was not part of a sustained personal interest in peas-

[27] Rosen, Judith, *Grażyna Bacewicz: Her Life and Works*. Polish Music History Series Vol. 2. (Los Angeles: Friends of Polish Music, 1984), p. 15.

ant culture but due to a socialist realist duty, folklore being syn-onymous with nationalism. In opposition to socialist realism, in the political climate of the time, formalism was the worst crime that could be committed and Lutosławski's First Symphony (1947) was the first important musical work to be accused of being 'for-malistic'. It was subsequently removed from the concert halls for a number of years.[28] Once again, yet for different reasons, "the uni-versal aspiration of composers of post-war Poland was to find 'a synthesis between a contemporary musical language and the ele-ments of native tradition within a framework of individual, stylis-tic categories.' "[29]

The holding of the International Festival of Contemporary Music in Warsaw in 1956 symbolised a new freedom under the more liberal Polish Communist Party. At the 1956 Festival and in sub-sequent years, Polish ears were opened to Western trends in mod-ern music when the works of the Second Viennese School were heard for the first time. These avant-garde developments did not go unnoticed and presented a wealth of potentially inspiring ma-terial for young composers. At the time that Bacewicz was writing her Sixth Quartet (1960) she spoke about the dilemma:

> I want to maintain certain sections in the serial technique, but by the same token I want to give them a different character. I am not interested in pointillism because I believe the road to be too narrow, but I feel directed by the coloring in sounds and the new rhythms of electronic music.[30]

She explained that the reason she was drawn to serial tech-nique was in order to learn "a new rigor of form, a new discipline which would be far more attractive than the conventionalised dis-cipline of the tonal world".[31] In the same year it was written, the Polish critic Tadeusz Zieliński described the Quartet as "a work of great invention and interesting imagination, and at the same time a demonstration of impressive technical and construction

[28] *Ibid.*, p. 22.
[29] *Ibid.*, pp. 22-23.
[30] *Ibid.*, pp. 31-32.
[31] Le Page, Jane Weiner, 'Grażyna Bacewicz: Composer, Virtuoso Violinist, Pianist' *'Women Composers, Conductors, and Musicians of the Twentieth Century: Selected Bibliographies*, vol. 3. (Metchuen, N.J.: Scarecrow, 1988), p. 8.

craftmanship. Surely we have not heard such an excellent quartet since the times of Szymanowski!"[32] The boldness of her modern style is even more outspoken in the internationally acclaimed Seventh Quartet (1965). The same Polish critic described it as "a masterpiece of contemporary quartet literature"[33] and in a review of the piece in 1969 Lutosławski said:

> The String Quartet no. 7 is new evidence of the use of certain possibilities that have been hidden in this type of an ensemble, but which have never been utilized. From the time of Bartók very few composers have written in the same manner as Bacewicz who was able to penetrate the secrets of the string quartet.[34]

Despite these qualities of the last quartets Bacewicz followed a different path from that of her contemporaries, Penderecki and Lutosławski, who also wrote string quartets in the early sixties. In their various ways Penderecki and Lutosławski bring into question the role of conventional notation. Krzysztof Penderecki (b. 1933) also focuses on the perception of time and extended instrumental techniques which have provoked startled responses from music critics. His *Threnody 'To the Victims of Hiroshima'* (1960) received a somewhat facetious review from Frank Howes, critic of *The Times*, who stated that the composer called upon his string players to do everything with their instruments "short of actually playing them"[35] – a comment that might easily be made of the string quartets.

In a more serious vein, Penderecki challenges the history of the string quartet by transforming it into a medium where sounds and textures are employed entirely for their own sake. No. 1 (1960) is a good example of the sophisticated new range of hitting, tapping, scraping, sliding and violent plucking effects Penderecki developed in his string writing at this time. A list of instructions at the front of the score explains the meaning of the novel symbols used to prescribe these methods of 'playing' and demonstrates the composer's refusal to admit a difference between sound and noise. These include instructions to:

> play between bridge and tailpiece (on one, two, three or four strings);

[32] *Ibid.*, p. 8.
[33] Rosen, Judith, *op. cit.*, p. 34.
[34] *Ibid.*, p. 34.
[35] Jacobson, Bernard, *A Polish Renaissance* (London: Phaidon Press, 1996), p. 147.

play on tailpiece; [for different percussive effects,] strike the strings with the open palm of the hand or fingers (*sul tasto*); strike the upper part of the sounding board of the violin with the nut [of the bow] or the finger-tips.[36]

The Second Quartet (1968) employs a similar repertoire of instrumental techniques as the First and even a few more (for example, demanding that players whistle and play at the same time in b. 3). All four players are required to be equally virtuosic.

Conventional ways of notating rhythm are made redundant. Instead Penderecki's graphic notation indicates the duration of the 'note' by the length of the horizontal line that follows it (see Example 3).

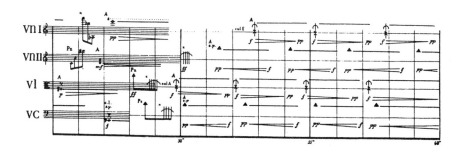

Ex. 3 Penderecki, String Quartet no. 1, 2'45" – 3'00"

There are no time signatures: in the First Quartet's single movement, conventional barlines are replaced by individual one-second sections that determine the tempo. Every five-second section is marked off by a thicker 'barline' within which the composer permits tempo deviations within the limits from 0.8 to 1.4 seconds, depending on the first violinist's choice.[37] In the Second Quartet the concept of time is even more fluid with no strict division of bars into seconds. But there is a more obvious arch-shaped structure, its single movement divided into three sections – *Lento molto*, *Vivace*, *Lento molto*.

In the First Quartet Penderecki uses pitch to help to define

---

[36] Penderecki, Krzysztof, *String Quartet* (New York: Belwin Mills, 1963). Preface to score.
[37] *Ibid.*

form: almost halfway through the piece (2'50" – 3'10") sounds of indeterminate pitch define a new section contrasting with the previous sections that comprise mostly exact pitches (see the extract in Example 3). While different widths of *vibrato* are specified in each quartet, the Second extends this pitch variation into a vertical dimension by building clusters in quarter-tones and semitones – a reference to the cluster techniques developed in *Threnody*. The opening cluster chord and the non-*vibrato/vibrato* effect recall Bartók's Third and Fourth Quartets respectively.

Despite Penderecki's adventurous experimentation, the homogeneity of the genre is not lost. His music is organised into blocks of sound distinguishable by their specific percussive sonorities and consistent or variable dynamic level. These blocks are usually defined by the vertical coincidence of gestures in different parts. Subsequent development grows from the increasing intensity and richness of diverse playing instructions. Thus timbre and texture have completely replaced thematic and motivic development.

Witold Lutosławski's (1913-1994) single String Quartet (1964) is a masterpiece of the repertoire in which sounds are similarly organised into blocks. However, his approach is very different from Penderecki's, as he applies his recently developed technique of aleatory counterpoint or, more specifically – since he does not apply it to all parameters but only to rhythm – limited aleatoricism. He emphasises the work's 'mobile' character as one of its most important features:

> a sequence of mobiles [...] are to be played one after another, without any pause if there is no other indication. Within certain points in time particular players perform their parts quite independently of each other. They have to decide separately about the length of pauses and about the way of treating ritenutos and accelerandos. However, similar material in different parts should be treated in a similar way.[38]

Vertical dotted lines indicate the places where players are required to begin together and a system of signals is written in the parts as cues. Contentious as these ideas may seem, the composer explained the purpose of his intentions thus:

---

[38] Excerpts from letters from Lutosławski to Walter Levin (first violinist of the La Salle Quartet) appear as a supplement to the score published by Chester.

It is not a question of diversity between performances; nor is it a question of the element of surprise; nor of freeing myself from part of the responsibility for the work and placing it on the performers. The aim of my endeavours has been merely to attain a certain definite sound result. This result is impossible to attain in any other way especially as regards rhythm and expression. I attach here a great importance to the influence of the musical text itself and explanatory notes for the performers.[39]

Lutosławski's way of ensuring the independence of parts was not to produce a full score. However, following correspondence with the La Salle Quartet who premiered the work, he reluctantly made a score available.

In response to the prevailing German influences, French composers provided a source of inspiration linking many Polish composers. Lutosławski likens his compositional aesthetic to Debussy's through the fact that

Debussy's system of organizing sound [that is, sensitivity to vertical aggregations] shows that he was indifferent to functions – that is what I have in common with him [...] Debussy organizes the sequence of chords in a very individual manner – and the need for an individual system is also something that makes me similar to him.[40]

These comments may be understood in relation to this piece if we consider the way that the relative functions of material have changed. This is one of the most explicit examples from the repertoire that shows how the traditional function of secondary parameters (such as dynamics, articulation, attack, timbre, texture) now take on the role of primary parameters (such as pitch, interval, rhythm) and vice versa.

Lutosławski's 'individual system' of organisation consists of related textural blocks of material.[41] Since there is no unifying pulse between the parts, there are no preconceived vertical coincidences. However, in the first movement of the Quartet, the recurring octave repetitions of the note C serve to punctuate the music and to

[39] Nordwall, Ove, (ed.), *Lutosławski* (Stockholm: Edition Wilhelm Hansen, 1968), p. 85.
[40] Varga, Bálint András, *Lutosławski Profile* (London: Chester, 1976), p. 17.
[41] See Coonrod, Michael McGill, 'Aspects of Form in Selected String Quartets of the Twentieth Century' DMA dissertation (Peabody Institute of the Johns Hopkins University, 1984), Chapter 3, 'Texture as Structure', pp. 95-125.

distinguish between textural, timbral and articulative changes in the score manifested in separate blocks or episodes (such as the *pizzicato* 'block' at Figure 5 or the legato trills at Figure 8 in the first movement). Eventually the octave C's undergo a transformation and are integrated into the form of the work. The vigorous *tremolando* figures that begin the second movement could be regarded as a development of the repeated C's (owing to the separate articulation of repeated notes) and are a recurring feature of the movement in different contexts. They reappear in their original octave form at Figure 39 but transformed into chords and played *pizzicato*.

Lutosławski's division of the work into two movements does not correspond to different characters and different tempi of traditional movements which, he explains, might be misleading. Instead he insists that the whole work is based on psychological development: "even music which contains strong contrasts can be closely knit through this inner 'psychological' development".[42] The observations above help to show not just psychological development but even 'motivic' development and the work's underlying unity where texture can now be defined as motivic.

Andrzej Panufnik's (1914-1991) music points in a different structural direction, based as it is on specifically geometric patterns. His adoption of highly controlled forms has, in general, been explained by Adrian Thomas as a consequence of the composer's "need to find and secure a compositional world that was safe from outside interference".[43] He experienced a long-term crisis following the onset of socialist realism in Poland and the cultural isolation resulting from his move to England in 1961.

The procedure of Panufnik's writing is not so different from Lutosławski's in the first section ('Prelude') of the First Quartet (1976) where he requires a relatively free, conversational manner of playing, *molto rubato*, which briefly returns at the beginning of the second and third sections. The homophonic texture of sustained notes in the 'extremely slow' second section ('Transformations') is coloured by a variety of dynamic and timbral contrasts

---

[42] Kaczyński, Tadeusz, *Conversations with Witold Lutosławski* (London: Chester, 1984), pp.18-19.
[43] Thomas, Adrian, 'Panufnik, Andrzej' in Sadie, Stanley (ed.), *op. cit.*, Vol. 19, p. 47.

while the 'very fast' third section ('Postlude') stresses the difference between the parts through their individually accented rhythms.

The Second Quartet, 'Messages', (1980) also focuses on specific sound qualities, initially creating a sparse texture of sustained harmonics. At the beginning, Panufnik requests that the four instruments should begin somewhere (unspecified) in the second half of the first bar so as to avoid any suggestion of simultaneity, as – in reverse – at the end. Tempo changes play a large part in determining different moods within the work's single movement. Its form and content have been designed around his childhood discovery of the sound of vibrating telephone wires, heard when putting his ear to the wooden telegraph poles.

The symmetrical paper-cuts made by peasants in northern Poland generate the image for the structure of the Third Quartet, 'Wycinanki' (1990). This image functions as a pattern for the articulation of musical material throughout the work.

Henryk Górecki's (b. 1933) approach to quartet writing explores sounds, textures and form from a less radical, though nonetheless interesting, perspective. In his two quartets – both written for the Kronos Quartet – 'Already it is Dusk' op. 62 (1988), and 'Quasi una fantasia' op. 64 (1991) – he relies on specifically tonal harmonies but uses them in unconventional ways. Rhythm and duration contribute more to the tension of the music than do harmonic progressions *per se* since Górecki uses bitonal harmonies as often in soft, sustained-note passages as in loud, rhythmically agitated and heavily accented ones. In 'Already it is Dusk', the melody is always placed in a dissonant context. Another side to Górecki's harmonic structures is that even where he does use tonal triads more often than not they are inverted so that we seldom observe conventional harmonic progressions.

'Quasi una fantasia' has four movements as opposed to the single-movement structure of 'Already it is Dusk' and their sources of inspiration are equally different: the latter is based on the four-part sixteenth-century Polish church song of the same title, whereas 'Quasi una fantasia' makes specific reference to Polish folk music with the folk string band implied in the second movement. Here, as elsewhere, the presence of a constant pulse is characteristic of Górecki's writing.

*

The two quartets of György Ligeti (b. 1923) were written within different traditions yet the composer acknowledges that "you can detect the sound of the First Quartet [1954], a much dissolved manifestation of it, in the Second [1968]".[44] The First Quartet, composed in Hungary and subtitled 'Métamorphoses nocturnes', continues in the vein of Bartók, especially noticeable in its textural and timbral devices. In an interview in 1978 Ligeti explains that "Bartók's sonorities were still valid for me, also his chromaticism, but I had to get beyond formal structure as used by Bartók, [...] not only the overall structural forms but also the small formal elements".[45] The main source material for this one-movement work is, however, an inital four-note motif (b. 7) which undergoes a variety of transformational techniques and is developed in different harmonic, rhythmic and textural contexts. It is in the Second Quartet that Ligeti more obviously departs from Bartók's compositional procedures, reflecting the developments of Ligeti's unique personal style in Vienna during the 1960s. The composer acknowledges that he "gradually evolved a musical style in which [he] abandoned structures conceived in terms of bars, melody lines and conventional forms". He says, "the thematic-motival structure and its role in the progress of music is almost completely abandoned. In this respect my Second String Quartet sums up all my previous work."[46]

Ligeti's preoccupations turn out to be similar to those of the Polish composers Penderecki and Lutosławski, where changes in timbre and texture replace thematic and motivic development. In a programme note for his orchestral piece *Atmosphères* (1961), Ligeti wrote that "timbre has a structural role in giving form to music".[47] He is perhaps less experimental in his exploration of timbre than Penderecki but blocks of timbre nevertheless dominate over harmony as the progressive element in the Second Quartet.

The Second Quartet is divided into five movements determined by five contrasting characters: "in the first movement the contrasting and fragmented type predominates, in the second the static

---

[44] Ligeti, György, with Péter Varnai, Josef Häuser and Claude Samuel, , *Ligeti in Conversation* (London: Eulenberg Books, 1983), p. 14.
[45] *Ibid.*, pp. 13-14.
[46] *Ibid.*, p. 14.
[47] *Ibid.*, p. 39.

character (*tenuto, legato*); in the third the mechanical form, in the fourth the threatening and brutal aspect, in the fifth a diatonic, surface *sonoro piano*."[48] The entire piece is structured on precise extremes in sonority, attack and dynamic, such as those witnessed in the opening bars.

Ligeti experiments with the relationship between pitch and timbre in the second movement where fluctuations in these elements are produced by means of different devices: a change in the position of the execution of the same note on different strings (indicated by roman numerals in the score); rapid alternation of different ways of producing the sound (*sul tasto, senza vibrato, flautando,* ordinary, *sul ponticello, vibrato*); microtonal inflections from b. 6. One apt description of the musical processes here is described by the German analyst, Harald Kaufmann as 'canon timbre'.[49] The seeming continuity of different strands of the 'canon timbre' is gradually intensified by changes in rhythm and sound quality which include prolonged trills and *tremolos*. Thus patterns in articulation define large portions of the music as well as small-scale surface colouring. The process of rhythmic fragmentation (which is not dissimilar to Bartók's compositional procedures) becomes accentuated by the alternation of dramatic methods of execution: *sul ponticello,* with *legno tratto, legno battuto, vibrato* and *tremolo,* ordinary *pizzicato* and *pizzicato secco,* and later, four different methods of *pizzicato.*

The composer's indications in the score are clear proof of his obsession with the idea of togetherness yet Ligeti's directions for *not* playing together are equally paramount. Leading to the climax of the third movement, at b. 25 he writes, "very precise: the demisemiquaver motion is simultaneous in all 4 instruments".[50] However, near the beginning of this movement (and elsewhere in the piece) rhythmically asynchronous passages demand that the four players persistently try to be independent of each other, although not in a loose context as, for example, in Lutosławski's

---

[48] Borio, Gianmario, 'L'eredità Bartókiana nel Secondo Quartetto di G. Ligeti: Sul Conceto di Tradizione nella Musica Contemporanea' ['The Legacy of Bartók in G. Ligeti's Second Quartet: On the Concept of Tradition in Contemporary Music'], trans. Rachel Fuller. *Studi Musicali* 13 (1984), p. 295.

[49] *Ibid.*, p. 298.

[50] Ligeti, György, *String Quartet no. 2* (Mainz: Schott, 1971), p. 18.

quartet. Here the boundaries of independence are very strict. Like many other mid- to late-twentieth-century works, Ligeti's Second Quartet effectively narrows the gap between notation and performance that exists for earlier repertoire. Players have very little, if any, interpretative licence because performance directions are the very essence of the work. The priority given to performance instructions throughout the piece, and their function in outlining formal structure, can be attributed to the continuity of the Bartók tradition.[51] But the fact that these markings are *so* specific in this piece makes it quite different from its predecessors and even more articulate than Penderecki's.

The innovative, expressive qualities of another Hungarian, György Kurtág (b. 1926), posit a different approach to quartet writing. His String Quartet op. 1 (1959), was written the year before the Sixth Quartet of Bacewicz and the First Quartet of Penderecki, and perhaps sits between the two in terms of its exploration of sound qualities within a framework based on the incorporation of traditional elements. Rather than relying on techniques of post-1945 serial music, Kurtág adopts some of the concision of Webern's own gestures, especially his condensed expression of abruptly contrasting registers, dynamics and timbre. Despite this influence, the fragmentation of Kurtág's brief melodic ideas is not necessarily the most striking feature of the work. For example, Stephen Walsh has observed "significant echoes of Bartók in the drastic opposition of different types of string articulation (*glissando*, *ostinato* clusters, *tremolando*, etc.)".[52] The form of the Quartet has also been attributed to Bartók's middle-period quartets "in the arch-like pairing of movements 1 with 6 and 2 with 5".[53]

The subsequent quartets were written some years later: *Hommage à Mihály András* (*12 Microludes for String Quartet*) op. 13 (1977), *Officium breve in memoriam Andreæ Szervánsky* op. 28 (1989), and *Aus der Ferne I* (1981), *II* (1986) and *III* (1991) in honour of publisher Alfred Schlee's eightieth, eighty-fifth and ninetieth birthdays. *Microludes* derives from the cycle of twelve 'microludes' in

---

[51] See Bayley, Amanda, 'Analysis of Bartók's String Quartet No.4, third movement: a new interpretative approach', *Music Analysis* 19/3 (2000), pp. 353-382.
[52] Walsh, Stephen, 'György Kurtág: an outline study (I)' in *Tempo* No. 140, March 1982, p. 13.
[53] Willson, Rachel Beckles, 'Kurtág, György' in Sadie, Stanley (ed.), *op. cit.*, Vol. 14, p. 45.

Játékok [Games] (1975-1998) for piano. These were originally written as didactic pieces for the piano studies of Kurtág's son. The *Microludes* for string quartet are similarly brief and extremely diverse, each movement associated with a specific pitch one semitone higher than the previous, and each pertaining to a particular character. Thus Kurtág applies a new idea to the string quartet, combining Webern's sense of exploiting a minute idea to the full, while adapting a keyboard idiom related to the idea of the Bagatelle or Bartók's *Mikrokosmos*.

Officium breve in memoriam Andreæ Szervánsky (1989) is based on a similarly miniature idea consisting of fifteen movements. It is a memorial to the Hungarian composer, Szervánsky, to Webern and to four other of Kurtág's friends listed at the front of the score. The dramatic contrasts between movements (which reflect the diverse musical styles of these composers) are set up through a mosaic of arrangements of Szervánsky's music, Webern's *Kantate II* op. 31 (1943), and Kurtág's own works. The piece ends with the first twelve bars of Szervánsky's *Arioso* (1948) which breaks off suddenly, leaving a visually and aurally incomplete work: "the poignancy of the interruption is compounded by the listener's mistaken assumption that, in the medium of the string quartet above all, Kurtág's musical dichotomies will be woven into a satisfying conclusion".[54]

*

From the time of Janáček it can be seen how Kodály, Enescu, Szymanowski, Bartók, Martinů, Bacewicz and Górecki have variously made folk music an integral part of their musical language and that folk music is the common denominator between these otherwise diverse composers. Apart from Górecki, all these composers adopt thematic contrasts to outline their forms in place of tonal contrasts and Janáček, Bartók, Martinů and Bacewicz rely even more heavily on textural changes. Bartók's legacy constantly surfaces both in the context of his contemporaries and his successors. He demonstrates the most highly developed thematic, harmonic and rhythmic ideas from the synthesis of art music and folk music, in addition to innovative textures and instrumental techniques, as inspiration for the next generation of composers. However, broader European influences also play an important part in the music of all Central European composers post-1945. Of these Hába follows an individualistic route along a microtonal path that seems to lead nowhere, Panufnik seeks constant renewal in forms as well as textures, and Górecki seeks inspiration further back in time and 're-invents' tonality to suit his own expressive ends. So many forms, methods of rhythmic organisation, and sound sources (chromatic harmonies, modalities, tone clusters, isolated pitches, quarter tones, percussive sounds) are available to composers that any generalisation fails.

In the 1960s, avant-garde developments in Europe are evident in the quartets of Penderecki, Lutosławski and Ligeti. They all use blocks of sounds and contrasting sonorities to articulate their musical structures and to prioritise changes in timbre and texture above traditional elements of melody and harmony. Despite their different attitudes towards notation and performance, they have arrived at similar expressive conclusions, especially concerning aspects of rhythm, timbre and texture. Each of these composers has also found his own way to develop individual soloistic lines whose points of coincidence determine the structure of the music and they come closest to challenging the conventional role of players in a string quartet.

Both Penderecki and Lutosławski require four equally virtuosic players though Penderecki takes this a stage further, not only asking them to tap their instruments in different ways and in different places, but also to sustain a whistled note while playing. Lutosławski and Ligeti change the fundamental communication between players requiring them to avoid rhythmic unison except where specified. Ligeti devises an anti-ensemble technique in his Second Quartet (yet, conversely, asks that the players articulate fast-moving passages "as though the four instruments were a single instrument"[55]). Right from the outset Lutosławski allows each player to play rhythmically and expressively but freely, yet he too requires some ensemble communication requesting players to signal to the others

---

[55] Ligeti, György, *op. cit.*, p. 27.

that each has finished a particular section – for example, see Figures 15 and 16 in the second movement). Lutosławski appears to challenge the conventional idea of the full interdependence of parts yet clearly the piece would not work if the players adopted entirely soloistic roles without a controlled framework. As he explains: "The idea behind a 'collective *ad libitum*' music is to transpose all the richness of solo playing into the field of ensemble music."[56]

While such independent playing techniques have developed through the medium of the string quartet, they clearly confront the aesthetic of an established tradition. Broadly speaking there is no longer a leader nor any perceptible hierarchy between instruments, but a consistently close integration of parts (even in Lutosławski) means that the genre of the string quartet nevertheless still fits firmly within the traditional framework of chamber music.

[I would like to express my gratitude to Susan Bradshaw for reading and commenting on an early draft of this chapter.]

[56] Nordwall, Ove (ed.), *op. cit.*, p. 86.

IV

The Soviet and Russian Quartet

Alan George

In November 1976 the Fitzwilliam String Quartet was invited to play in the USSR. A visit had earlier been fixed with Dmitri Shostakovich himself for September the previous year, when we were going to stay in his *dacha* and work with him on a pre-arranged selection of his quartets and, following his death in August 1975, his widow Irina Antonovna still wanted us to come for a concert tour.

On the last day of our trip, following a riotous overnight train journey from Leningrad on the Red Arrow, we were lavishly entertained by the Union of Soviet Composers, which boasted a membership of several thousand. It was salutary to discover that in the Soviet Union creative artists were not treated as third-class citizens, begging performers and promoters alike to put on their music. Their works were published and recorded as a matter of course. This, it has to be said, resulted in an unwieldy body of material of alarmingly variable quality, but at least the opportunity was there for everything to be heard and judged.

Seated around a table with a dozen or so of the country's leading creative musical minds, we were treated to recordings of a string quartet by each of them and received gifts of their scores, all (with one exception) neatly bound and printed. Two figures in particular excited us. One was Boris Tchaikovsky (1925-99), whom Shostakovich himself had warmly recommended to us as one of his most gifted pupils and whose Quartet no. 3 of 1967 proved to be a finely constructed work in six movements, beautifully conceived for the medium and truly haunting in its impact. The other was Alfred Schnittke (1934-98) who made an even greater impression.

His contribution was a brief Canon composed in 1971 in memory of Igor Stravinsky and perhaps inspired by Stravinsky's own choice of this form thirteen years earlier for his memorial to the painter Raoul Dufy (the *Double Canon* for string quartet). What Schnittke gives us in this piece is, in effect, a single line of music, with each player moving in succession from one note to the next (hence the description 'canon'), thereby creating a series of blurred, constantly shifting harmonies. We were mesmerised by this little epigram which proved by far the most striking and memorable music we heard that day. The Fitzwilliam Quartet was able to give the piece its Western premiere not long afterwards and, along with our former colleague Professor David Blake, developed a personal friendship with Schnittke who was our guest at York University for a few days in May 1979.

Schnittke was probably the youngest of the composers present at that meeting and represented a marked turning away from the post-Shostakovich idiom from which so many of his older colleagues seemed unable to break free. Indeed, at the time he was not at all accepted by the Soviet establishment (it was his score – unprinted and on a single hand-written sheet – that was the aforementioned exception). Since then, of course, he has become one of the best known of all late-twentieth-century composers.

Schnittke's First Quartet dates from 1966 but it was with the Piano Quintet of 1976 that he truly found his voice in the world of the string quartet (and as such it occupies a similar position to that of Shostakovich's Piano Quintet). A profoundly moving requiem for his mother, the work conveys an acute sense of grief, pain and tears through the judicious use of quarter-tones and string textures that are reminiscent of Shostakovich at his most anguished. The Quartet no. 3, composed in 1983 for the Manhattan Society for New Music, is entirely characteristic of his highly personal and eclectic language, employing an almost Ivesian collage technique in which quotations from Lassus, Beethoven and Shostakovich are woven effortlessly into the musical fabric.

Although virtually all the best-known Russian quartets are by composers who are no longer alive (and, with his death, Schnittke's canon of quartets joins that succession), a possible exception might be thought to be Sofia Gubaidulina (b. 1931) who has recently been making a considerable impact in the West. Her Quartet no. 3 (1987), which opens with a strikingly bold demonstration of the effectiveness of harmonics and *pizzicati*, is particularly impressive. It is fervently to be hoped that works like the Gubaidulina will quickly establish themselves in the repertoire, since there are, in fact, not many Russian quartets to choose from – a situation that, perhaps, requires a little explanation.

The greatest nineteenth-century examples of Russian quartets are undoubtedly those by Borodin and Tchaikovsky (a grand total of five and a quarter), but those of Borodin were frowned on by his nationalist colleagues in the 'Moguchaya Kuchke' ['The Mighty Handful'], while Tchaikovsky listed chamber works with strings as among his most hated instrumental combinations. There was a strong enthusiasm among amateurs (typified by the Friday quartet meetings at the home of Belaiev and his subsequent publication of various short pieces in two volumes appropriately entitled *Les vendredis*), but it has to be admitted that the great Russian composers were temperamentally more suited to the scale and dramatic scope of opera and the symphony. Borodin's Quartet no. 2 and Tchaikovsky's First Quartet are familiar enough (or, at least, their slow movements are – in whatever arrangement) but how often does one hear Tchaikovsky's Second and Third Quartets? Can no. 2 really be Borodin's only quartet?

Alexander Glazunov (1865-1936) and Sergei Taneyev (1856-1915), two fine composers who contributed abundantly to the literature, had feet in both the Tsarist and Soviet eras. Between them they produced thirteen quartets (plus another five by Taneyev that remain unpublished), and various smaller works for the medium. In many ways it was these works, perhaps more than those of their illustrious predecessors, that exerted the greater influence on the quartet writing of the Soviet period, through their demonstration of how to write most idiomatically and resourcefully for four string instruments. Sergei Prokofiev (1891-1953) and Igor Stravinsky (1882-1971) also spanned both centuries but showed far less prowess with the medium. Indeed, in *The String Quartet – A History*, Paul Griffiths claims that Stravinsky's *Three Pieces* of 1913 are "for the first time in the history of the genre, determinedly not 'a string quartet' but a set of pieces to be played by four strings".[1] Similarly Stravinsky's *Concertino* (1920) defies the line of development by promoting the first violin to the role of soloist, as implied by the title of the work. Apart from the *Double Canon in memoriam Raoul Dufy*, Stravinsky found no more use for the string quartet other than in the context of a larger chamber ensemble.

At least Prokofiev, if hardly more prolific than Stravinsky in this area, recognized that the string quartet had a part to play in his

---

[1] Griffiths, Paul, *The String Quartet – A History* (London: Thames and Hudson, 1983), p. 170.

country's new musical heritage. The second of his two quartets (op. 92 in F major) even looks back to Haydn in its embracing of folk material to increase popular appeal, perhaps, as Paul Griffiths suggests, acknowledging Socialist Realism's eschewing of musical revolution in favour of the "safety of traditional moulds".[2]

Dmitri Shostakovich, who was writing his own Quartet no. 2 at the same time as Prokofiev, would choose an entirely different path. The rest of this chapter will be devoted to the tremendous legacy that he bequeathed to the genre.

By the time Shostakovich came to write his First Quartet at the age of thirty-two, his chamber output consisted of no more than a piano trio, three pieces for cello and piano, two pieces each for string octet and string quartet and a sonata for cello and piano. Was he, perhaps, deliberately avoiding the string quartet medium? We are reminded of Sibelius, who refrained from writing a symphony until he had reached op. 39, or Brahms, who was so aware of the shadow of Beethoven that his first symphony was delayed until he had reached op. 68 and was only shortly preceded by his first string quartet op. 51 (and both works in the stormy Beethovenian key of C minor). Perhaps Shostakovich, whose first quartet was op. 49, was also affected by an awareness of the achievement of Beethoven.

During his early manhood, Shostakovich was greatly influenced by a whole amalgam of art and history, not the least element of which was his consciousness of his own native musical heritage. Russia, as we have seen, had always lacked a strong quartet tradition. Shostakovich was single-handedly to change that aspect of musical history (witness the hundreds of quartets turned out by hundreds of composers since, most of which clearly demonstrate their debt to the Shostakovich canon). For many years, however, the wide-spread championing of Shostakovich's quartets in his native land was only sporadically reflected in the West where many ensembles seemed oddly reluctant to admit them into the hallowed, exclusive standard quartet repertoire (apart, that is, from the Eighth Quartet, and one suspects that the extra-musical associations implicit in this work had a hand in that). Happily this state of affairs has gradually changed, as the critical and popular response has become ever-more vociferous.

[2] *Ibid.*, p. 212.

The quartets are always likely to be less generally familiar than the symphonies and it is tempting to treat the series of symphonies and the series of quartets as representing respectively the public and private sides of Shostakovich's artistic nature. It is a view that the composer opposed passionately and indeed, while such comparison demonstrates a gradual shift of emphasis from one genre to another – after the end of the war he composed six symphonies and thirteen quartets whereas before that time he had to his credit nine symphonies but only two quartets – the division between the two is only skin deep, since the earlier quartets tend to be symphonic in conception while the last symphonies tend to become more rarefied and inward-looking. Yet the dedications on the quartets' scores do testify to an intimacy that is very much in tune with the spirit of chamber music, since all are dedicated to close personal acquaintances including his two wives as well as the members of the Beethoven Quartet, the ensemble that premiered all but the first and the last. Curiously enough, while the symphonies tend to favour the minor keys, the quartets reveal a preponderance of major keys and it was not until the Seventh that Shostakovich chose a minor key for a quartet (although the existing ratio of ten major to five minor keys would have been rectified had he lived longer, since in the early '60s he hit on the idea of writing a quartet in each of the twenty-four keys – a clearly-ordered scheme that can be traced from no. 8 onwards).

Since there is no full length 'early' quartet by Shostakovich, it is both possible and desirable to divide the series into two groups corresponding to the familiar 'middle' and 'late' period divisions allotted to the works of composers such as Beethoven and Mahler. The division is by no means an equal one, nor is it particularly clear-cut, but the last four do seem to belong so much together that they must be seen slightly apart from the rest. The first eleven quartets, inevitably, represent a more varied experience. They tend to be more outward-looking and, although hardly without their moments of sadness and melancholy, they are often robust and even light-hearted and reveal a basic allegiance to the principles of Classical form and structure allied to a never-failing grasp of what constitutes truly idiomatic quartet writing. Unlike Beethoven and Bartók, Shostakovich never really sought to strain the medium beyond its already existing limits; instead, he accepted the medium for what it was and gradually refined and sublimated it. In this respect he can hardly be considered to have expanded the technique of string quartet writing: whether or not he increased its expressive range is a different matter.

So, what do they sound like, these quartets? Perhaps the first impression (unless one is listening to the more dense areas of such pieces as no. 2 and no. 5) is of a certain restraint and economy of scoring. For the most part, the instrumental writing is pleasantly idiomatic and, for the performers, eminently satisfying to play. Indeed, perhaps more than any composer since Mozart, Shostakovich has contributed a body of quartet music that is accessible to amateurs and young students, to whom can be confidently recommended whole movements of Quartets nos. 1, 4 and 6-11. The instruments are used equally effectively as both soloists and as constituents of an ensemble, and are rarely required to indulge in tricks or effects other than *pizzicato* (although there are *pizzicato* passages in Quartets nos. 6 and 9 that are truly awesome in their dramatic power and in which the players have to be prepared to risk breaking every string on their instruments). Mutes are also frequently employed and provide the primary colour at the end of no less than ten of the quartets. *Sul ponticello* appears on just two occasions (in nos. 10 and 12); *col legno* not once. Mention must also be made of the percussive taps in the central section of Quartet no. 13, where the bellies of the three lower instruments are hit softly with the tip of the bow. People often ask what these taps mean or whether we, as members of the Fitzwilliam Quartet, asked Shostakovich why he put them there. We didn't question him (although we did joke with him that the leader of the Beethoven Quartet, Dmitri Tsyganov, must have had a more expensive instrument than his colleagues); as for any dramatic or philosophical explanation, I can only say that the passage sounds far less effective without them.

What is noticeable about the Shostakovich sound is that his textures seem unerringly geared towards the type of acoustic for which they were conceived: spacious, warm, rich, clear and with just enough resonance to enable the biggest moments to sound almost orchestral and provide a supportive glow around the merest whisper of sound. Every single hall in Russia in which the Fitzwilliam Quartet has played has ideal acoustics (at least until recently: the little concert hall in the Pushkin House in St. Petersburg is miserably hard work). This is no better demonstrated than by the Glinka Hall, the small hall of the Phiharmonia in St. Peters-burg.[3] The Wigmore Hall in London, rightly famous for its quali-ties, comes nearest to the sonic splendour of a Russian hall. Such venues enable the enormous range of Shostakovich's textures to make their impact most tellingly.

Shostakovich's harmonic language was basically tonal (at least, it was by the time he came to writing the quartets), although this is not to suggest an absence of a level of dissonance commensurate with his being a twentieth-century composer. In the first eleven quartets he achieves dissonance in a number of ways. Firstly, he simply lines up pitches which together form an obviously violent clash (witness the more aggressive movements of Quartets nos. 8 and 10, or the deliberately nasty chord that supports the violin recitative at the beginning of Quartet no. 11). The norm of disso-nance can also be surprisingly high in some of the more knotty fugal or contrapuntal passages, where Shostakovich is clearly think-ing about the horizontal lines, irrespective of the resulting har-monic clashes. Occasionally also, as in Quartets nos. 3 and 5, he pits two keys against one another. At the end of the second move-ment of Quartet no. 3, for example, the cello rhapsodises in a mixture of keys but the supporting harmony is unequivocally E minor. The resulting polytonality gives rise to a strange dissonance all of its own.

Just as the harmonic language in these quartets is essentially tonal, so is the melodic style inherently diatonic. The richness and variety of Shostakovich's melodies bear witness to his exceptional affinity with the human voice and its capabilities as an instrument of high drama or poignant tenderness. It would not be an exag-geration to claim that, like most of his great predecessors (notably Mussorgsky, Borodin and even Tchaikovsky), Shostakovich felt most at home in the theatre. The infamous scandal surrounding *Lady Macbeth of Mtsensk*, however – when *Pravda* denounced the opera as "chaos instead of music" – deprived him not only of per-sonal safety and a secure state of mind, but also of the opera thea-tre. After the *Lady Macbeth* affair, Shostakovich never again had the confidence to complete a full-length opera and, although he

[3] A recent concert there – experienced from the stalls – suggests, however, that something has changed.

continued to produce a huge amount of incidental music and many film scores, thereafter his inherent feeling for the voice and the theatre found outlet in his instrumental music – witness not only the unusual frequency of instrumental recitatives in his symphonies and quartets but also the truly 'singable' quality of so much of his melodic writing. Even when Shostakovich resorts to the deliberately trivial, in the biting ironic manner so tellingly employed by one of his great heroes, Gustav Mahler (as at the opening of Quartet no. 3), one can still sing it, just as one can sing such a poignant cantilena as that given to the first violin in the *Adagio* of Quartet no. 10, a prime example of his deeply moving use of expressively chromatic lines to heighten emotional intensity. The harmonic and melodic language of the last four quartets, and also their special approach to structure, require separate discussion, however, and will be dealt with later.

It has sometimes been cruelly said of the Shostakovich quartets that he was merely writing the same piece over and over again (such criticisms have also been made of other significant bodies of music, of Bruckner's symphonies, for example). While such a view takes little account of anything we have observed about these works so far, it could be said that various structural characteristics do indeed appear with a certain frequency. One might summarise the four characteristic movement types in Shostakovich's quartets thus:

i) First Movements:
First movements are invariably in sonata form or a variant of it, although rarely traditional sonata *Allegros* (Shostakovich's oft-expressed frustration at his failure to produce a true symphonic *Allegro* is well documented – perhaps he had forgotten the first movement of Quartet no. 5). The fugato-based movement that opens Quartet no. 8 is an exception to this generalisation but even so, apart from the single-movement Quartet no. 13, sonata form still influences even the last quartets.

ii) Slow Movements:
Many of the slow movements are freely rhapsodic (Quartets nos. 2, 4, 8, 9, 11), although the rhapsodic approaches something more definable in Quartets nos. 5 and 7. Quartet no. 1 has a simple set of variations, a form that develops into the more rigorous *passacaglia* in Quartets nos. 3, 6 and 10 – in all three of which the *passacaglia* ground theme reappears in the finale to crown the moment of

climax. It is, however, the instrumental recitatives which form the most adventurous and pioneering contributions to the slow movement forms. In both Quartets nos. 2 and 11 we find complete movements headed *Recitative*, the earlier work in particular challenging the player's technique and powers of imagination by presenting them with an unprecedented degree of what one might call 'controlled improvisation'. A further example appears at a point of high drama in the fourth movement of Quartet no. 9 while, as I shall discuss later, the whole concept of increased freedom of individual expression is taken a stage or two further in the last four quartets.

iii) Scherzi:
The most usual scherzo type is the waltz, a dance that may have had its origins in pre-Strauss Vienna but had already cross-bred with the minuet and the German dance and Ländler as far back as Haydn, Mozart and Beethoven (witness the opp. 130 and 132 Quartets). A similar cross-breeding also occurs in the *Alla Tedesca* second movement of Tchaikovsky's Third Symphony and it is surely the ease and frequency with which, in Tchaikovsky's hands, from the First Symphony onwards, the scherzo can metamorphose into the waltz that inspired Shostakovich to continue this tradition. Waltzes appear somewhere in most of Shostakovich's quartets – explicitly in Quartet no. 2, implicitly in Quartets nos. 1 and 6 (and even no. 4) and with heavy irony in Quartets nos. 3 and 8. The dance element is developed further to form the finales of Quartets nos. 5 and 7 (and, stretching a point, no. 9) and yet further in various passages in nos. 12, 14 and 15. The other important scherzo species which abounds in both the symphonies and the quartets is the wild, relentlessly aggressive type found in Quartets nos. 3, 7, 8 and 10. Here, more than anywhere else in the quartets (with the exception of the first movements of nos. 2 and 5), is Shostakovich straining for an orchestral scale and sonority, and yet he exploits the quartet so skilfully that he secures the greatest possible sonic impact without there being any sense of his being frustrated by the medium. Whilst such movements are no less common in the symphonies (in Symphonies nos. 8 and 10, for example), the kind of Mahlerian scherzo found in Symphonies nos. 5 and 6 reached the recital room only in Shostakovich's chamber works with piano – the Cello Sonata and the Piano Quintet – not in the quartets, an omission that is perhaps explained by the

fact that this type of movement only seemed to hold a real interest for him for a period of just six years. A further type of scherzo can be found in Quartets nos. 1, 4 and 9, deft character-pieces of a playful, whimsical nature in which mutes are employed to exploit the more shadowy regions of the quartet sonority. The example in Quartet no. 9 is reputed to have been the composer's own favourite; perhaps it conceals something especially personal to do with its dedicatee, Shostakovich's wife Irina Antonovna.

iv) Finales:

From Quartet no. 3 onwards (excluding, of course, the last four quartets) virtually all the finales are easy-paced sonata rondos, most of them rising to a mighty climax and eventually dying away into silence. The principle exceptions are the noisy *Allegros* of Quartets nos. 1 and 9 and the finales of Quartets nos. 7, 8 and 11, where their cyclic structures and deliberately elegiac subject matter inevitably demanded something more personal. The tremendous set of variations which concludes Quartet no. 2 is unique, one of the most resourceful and exciting of all Shostakovich's finales which ingeniously increases the pulse through successive groups of variations while simultaneously contriving to build a gigantic arch form that moves from slow to fast music and back to slow again. In every one of his quartets, Shostakovich found a way of reaching the end of the work in such a way as to leave the listener totally absorbed by the journey experienced. The "problem of the finale", which so bedevilled composers after Beethoven, is totally solved by looking at the identity of each work and finding an appropriate and individual conclusion.

*

It is pertinent at this point to dwell for a moment on the nature of Shostakovich's quartets as works to be performed, rather than as scores sitting on a library shelf. I have looked at the sound world which these quartets inhabit, but how is this best realised to ensure that the listener has a true and faithful glimpse into that peculiarly personal region? The first rule in performing these works is to play exactly what the composer wrote. This is especially crucial with Shostakovich since what he actually notates is so very simple and explicit that not every performer really trusts what is there on the page. Shostakovich's is a sound world of its own and, of course, one that the elder generation of Russian quartets can immediately identify with. It was essential for us, in the Fitzwilliam Quartet, to study this school of playing since, while a British quartet can no more transfuse Russian blood into their veins than they can speak the Russian language without a trace of an English accent, it is entirely possible and desirable in order to understand how these Russian players produced their individual sound. At the gathering at the Union of Soviet Composers mentioned at the beginning of this chapter, we were fortunate enough to meet Dmitri Tsyganov, the leader of the Beethoven Quartet, who explained his own, instantly recognisable sound as emanating from the teaching of Leopold Auer and its emphasis on an 'economical' style of bowing allied to a rhythmically disciplined *vibrato*.

That may be the basis of the Beethoven Quartet's sound, but it is nothing without the application of boundless imagination, an imagination arrived at by thorough study of the scores and a grasp of the 'orchestration' implied at any given moment. Thus, for example, however disciplined the vibrato, the variety of its use is no less crucial: there are so many places where a varied use can realize the amazing colours already implicit in the music (see, as an example, the *Andante* of Quartet no. 5).

Articulation and note lengths are as important, their notation being rather more explicit than many players can bring themselves to believe. In his essay on performing these quartets, Christopher Rowland, the former leader of the Fitzwilliam Quartet, is at pains to point out that when Shostakovich wants the notes to be played short, off the string, he indicates this precisely; when he does not, then something else is required – too many players today are reluctant to play on the string, truly *legato* as Russians like (or used to like) to do.[4] Dr. Rowland also discusses at length one of the more vexing aspects of performing these (or any) works. Tempo will invariably provoke more argument than most matters of interpretation, but in the case of Shostakovich we have not only the composer's metronome markings but also his recorded performances with which comparisons can be (and in Dr. Rowland's essay are, extensively,) made. Over the years, the Fitzwilliam Quartet's approach to the composer's tempo markings has, if anything, be-

---

[4] Rowland, Christopher, in *Shostakovich: the Man and His Music*, ed. Christopher Norris (London: Lawrence and Wishart Ltd., 1982).

come more rigorous, the experience of performing the quartets in all manner of venues proving that the notated tempo indications usually do work rather well. That is not to say that a degree of intelligent flexibility is out of place; indeed, we can learn from Shostakovich's own playing that such a flexibility is entirely authentic. Intelligence is also called for in those rare situations where a miscalculation really does seem to have occurred as, for example, in the Valse of Quartet no. 2 and the *Lento* of no. 6 (for the latter of which the tempo adopted by the Fitzwilliam Quartet had the composer's direct approval).

*

We must now cross the threshold into the peculiarly withdrawn world of the four last quartets.

If one hears someone use the phrase 'the late quartets' it is likely that they will be referring to Beethoven (or possibly Schubert, if anything written by a man under thirty-one can possibly be construed as 'late'). With Mozart we talk about 'the Prussian quartets', with Haydn 'the op. 76 and op. 77', but otherwise no composer of comparable stature has produced enough quartets to necessitate a division into groups. But over the last thirty years or so, people have referred to 'the late quartets' of Shostakovich, and there are two very pertinent reasons for that. In fact, like Beethoven's, Shostakovich's career as a whole falls conveniently into three periods, although identifying the division between the second and third is complicated by the fact that the quartets tended to appear at regular intervals. A comparison between the end of Quartet no. 11 (Example 1a) and the beginning of no. 12 (Example 1b) is revealing:

Ex. 1a Quartet no. 11, final 12 bars

Ex. 1b Quartet no. 12, first 12 notes

The opening of Quartet no. 12 is obviously less tonally orientated than the end of no. 11. At the end of no. 11 we have twelve bars of pure F minor; at the beginning of no. 12 a simple, unashamed twelve-note row – it could almost be Schoenberg. In the light of Shostakovich's supposedly reactionary attitude to one of the twentieth century's great innovators, this marks a fairly adventurous step forward on the composer's part, but it was as far as he was prepared to go – for the time being. The last two notes of the row make a perfect cadence into D flat and thereafter the music remains firmly in that key for the rest of the first subject group. The opening of Quartet no. 13 (see Example 2) provides another instance of what we might call a 'tonal note-row' – an idea that Shostakovich may have got from Berg, a composer whom he revered. In this case we have four different notes (the first three forming a triad), which are then repeated a semitone lower to give, in all, the first eight notes of a row. The only ambiguity here is whether we are in D flat major or B flat minor. But then the last four of the twelve notes, followed by four that have already been used, effect a modulation into C with, in the passage that follows, this C acting not so much as a tonal centre but more like a melodic pivot:

Ex. 2 Quartet no. 13, opening to Figure 2

Unlike Schoenberg or Berg, Shostakovich never used a twelve-note row as the basis for a serial composition but he did make an effort to break free from the comfort and safety of purely tonal composition. The function of these rows, in works that are still fundamentally tonal, is to establish a conflict between tonality and atonality and nowhere is the conflict more violent than in the first movement of Quartet no. 12 . Having been used extensively in Quartets nos. 12 and 13, in the Violin Sonata and in Symphonies nos. 14 and 15, such rows gradually appear less frequently, or rather less obviously, but the musical language remains essentially the same in the subsequent works: the technique had clearly exerted so profound an influence on his harmonic and melodic thinking that Shostakovich no longer found it necessary to use all twelve notes in succession in order to combat tonality. There is nothing particularly revolutionary in Shostakovich's toying with twelve-note rows, nor was he trying out something new merely for the sake of it (note rows were hardly new in 1968). Rather, he was allowing his feelings and his instincts to find their own means of expression, as was so often his method, and these final works demonstrate total assurance and mastery in their command of language and content. They reveal a few surprises as well, none more so than in the following dense pile-up of note rows from Quartet no. 12 (see Example 3), the identity of the composer of which might, on a 'blind' hearing, cause some difficulty:

Ex. 3 Quartet no. 12, Figures 33-34

One striking feature of the last quartets is their scoring. Although it is clear from the very beginning that it was not in Shostakovich's nature to expand the scope and technique of the medium, there are passages in the early quartets where he achieves an almost orchestral sonority. Such a sound hardly ever occurs in the last three quartets and in no. 15, in particular, there is not the merest trace. At the same time, the rarified textures which were never exactly unusual in Shostakovich's earlier quartets, become increasingly persistent until in no. 15 we are confronted with vast stretches of music for one instrument only. In the light of this it is not surprising to find that the last two symphonies, clearly affected by the writing of the quartets, are conceived very much in chamber style. In these last works that supposed division between 'public' and 'private' music has finally disappeared.

The other factor which all these late works share is their oppressively dark, gloomy and often frighteningly bleak nature. The Russian artistic temperament has, of course, always had a tendency towards morbidity; one has only to think of Mussorgsky, Tchaikovsky and Gogol and other great nineteenth-century writers, and a similar melancholy streak can be detected in much of

Shostakovich's work. One might, indeed, almost believe that his musical reaction to tragedy was more eloquent and sincere than his response to triumph. Shostakovich never enjoyed a particularly strong constitution and, with heart trouble, a stroke and a road accident, his health suffered badly during his last few year. Rejecting religion in any accepted sense, Shostakovich's terror of approaching death – founded on the concept of it being simply the end of life, the final and conclusive completion of existence – became an obsession from which he seemed unable to break free, and this reveals itself most in these last compositions.

It seems to me that the emotional origins of the blackness which pervades these final works go back to Quartet no. 7, composed in 1960 in memory of his first wife, Nina Vasilyevna, which, although by no means his first death-haunted composition, could well have been the first which had a lasting influence on his later musical language. Nina had actually died six years earlier and this delayed reaction seems to be a sign of a gradual withdrawal into himself, with the music becoming noticeably more introspective and, in many places (see, for example, the passage from five bars after Figure 18 to Figure 21) full of the sparse textures that foreshadow the late quartets. Quartet no. 7 is a strangely brief, seemingly unimportant, little piece but it was a crucially significant work for Shostakovich to have written. Certainly it was one of his favourites and he insisted that the Fitzwilliam Quartet play it to him when he visited us in York in 1972.

Quartet no. 7 explores new regions, as a delayed response to the new experience of a close personal bereavement, a bereavement closer than ever before. From this vantage point the late quartets can be viewed as a self-defining group that explores four entirely contrasting aspects of something common to them all – a 'new experience' the origins of which can clearly be traced back to eight years earlier. Whilst these four quartets can be seen to stand apart from their eleven predecessors, they should not be separated from the other major works of this final period of creativity. The Sonata for Violin and Piano op. 134 takes the language of Quartet no. 12 op. 133 a stage further; that of Symphony no. 14 op. 135 a stage further than that; there could be no more explicit exposition of the emotional world which this valedictory musical language inhabits than the eleven settings of poems, all of them on the subject of death, which form Symphony no. 14. The last symphony, Symphony no. 15, the last sonata (the Sonata for Viola and Grand Piano) and the last songs (*Suite on Verses of Michelangelo*) belong as much with the last quartets as the quartets belong with one another.

Yet the individual identity of the last four quartets should not be submerged by these close inter-relationships; there is no reason to suppose that they were at any time conceived as a group. Quartet no. 12 has to be regarded as the most positive of the four. It has just two movements, the second of which is extraordinarily wide-ranging and brings together a scherzo, slow movement, first movement recapitulation and finale into a single movement. Taken as a whole, this massive structure represents a titanic struggle between good and evil, optimism and pessimism, life and death, tonality and atonality. The outcome seems, to me, to be one of the most wildly joyful passages that Shostakovich ever wrote. Yet not everyone sees the Quartet in this way. For some, the end represents a desperate, manic struggle which is ultimately hollow and therefore depressing. As with so many of his earlier, apparently 'optimistic', conclusions there is an ambivalence, an ambiguity here – another example of Shostakovich speaking in opposites. Maxim Shostakovich has said:

> My father used the quartet genre for the deepest of his thoughts, for the expression of his most important philosophical conceptions. And in this category I would place the fifteen quartets as a lyrical confession of my father.[5]

Perhaps in the quartets we really should believe what we hear: each listener must make up his or her own mind.

After the end of Quartet no. 12 it is profoundly disturbing to find that its successor is one of the most depressing of experiences, ravaged as it is with anguish and despair. In no. 13 Shostakovich used the great second movement of its predecessor as a model and dispensed with the first movement altogether, leaving a single arch-like structure. The basic tempo is *Adagio* but its central section moves at exactly double the speed. Quite unlike anything else he

---

[5] Transcript from a speech at Bucknell University, USA, 13 September 1981, conferring honorary degrees on the members of the Fitzwilliam Quartet, reproduced in the programme booklet for the Quartet's complete Shostakovich cycle at Lincoln Center, New York, April / May, 1982.

wrote, this must be one of the strangest passages in all Shostakovich. It is dominated by a rhythmic motif that goes on and on – as does the *pizzicato* statement of the twelve-note row in the cello. For some listeners the intentional monotony might recall Sibelius's *Night-ride and Sunrise* and there is certainly something of the night here. It is here (Figure 19 to Figure 26) that those extraordinary percussive taps make their mark, emphasising the remorseless and inevitable tread of time (I've heard this referred to in Russia as a 'Dance of Death'). Towards the end, there is a heart-rending passage which suggests a final moment of consolation, but then the solo viola emerges and climbs higher and higher, as if to disappear, and finishes with the most awful shriek.

I have to admit that, when the set of hand-copied parts of Quartet no. 14 arrived from Moscow, and we in the Fitzwilliam Quartet first played it through, our reaction to the new quartet had already been influenced by the effect that no. 13 always had on us. Such passages as the light-hearted, Haydnesque opening seemed no more than a deceptive foil for those darker moments that we presumed to reveal the true nature of the work. But perhaps this jolly opening theme really is carefree and humorous, perhaps the intense climactic passage in the *Adagio* is not so much anguished and bitter but more passionate and radiant. Performers can (every now and then) listen with gratitude to what critics have to say and it was Joan Chissell who, at an early stage in the life of Quartet no. 14, put her finger on its essence when she described it as being "as deeply joyous as anything in Janáček's Indian summer".[6] Some people will disagree with such a strongly-expressed opinion but, in any case, it does the music no service at all to perform the work with leaden feet and a too-knowingly heavy heart. In spite of which, no. 14 is, without doubt, a predominantly serious work, the heart of which lies in its central *Adagio* and an unforgettable moment for all of us in the Fitzwilliam was our first encounter with the closing passage of this movement, one of the most beautiful and poignant in all chamber music, which reduced us all to silence for several minutes.

Quartet no. 14 is more traditional in design than no. 13 and marks an apparent regression from a rigorous self-contained struc-

---

[6] Talk on BBC Radio 3, 19 November 1975.

ture to a seemingly more diffuse three-movement layout. Yet the design of no. 14 bears more than a passing resemblance to that of no. 12 in that, after a free-standing first movement, the rest of the work unfolds in one continuous span in which the recapitulation of the second movement does not occur until after that of the third. A further overall unity originates in the repeated notes on the viola with which the work opens. These may seem, at first, to be no more than a formal call to attention, in preparation for the entry of the first subject on the cello, but their reappearance under various disguises at significant points in the course of the work confirms their structural importance and helps to dispel any superficial impression of diffuseness.

In each of the last four quartets, Shostakovich comes up with one or two totally novel ideas, all of which represent extensions of his musical vocabulary. The central section of no. 13 is a prime example. This is heralded by an extraordinary *Klangfarbenmelodie* [sound-colour melody] passage, a forerunner of a further exploitation of the Webern-associated technique in no. 14 (Figure 69 to Figure 73) where it is extended into a fierce 'slanging match' of over forty bars during which the players, in effect, hurl notes at each other. Quartet no. 14 contains an especially important part for the cello, an outcome of its dedication. Quartets nos. 11 to 14 were inscribed in turn to each of the original members of the Beethoven Quartet and the last to be so honoured was the cellist Sergei Petrovich Shirinsky (who, sadly, was not to live long enough to see the launching of no. 15). In no. 14, the cello is given an even more prominent role to play than the viola in no. 13 and, as in the 'Prussian' quartets of Mozart (which were also written for a cellist), textural equilibrium is considerably affected by this unusual balance of power with the viola, in particular, achieving a special independence because of its responsibility for holding a strongly supporting bass line. Shostakovich takes this individual prominence a stage further by presenting each player with almost complete freedom in recitative-like solo passages – passages in which the composer depends a great deal on the interpretative authority and instrumental command of the members of the quartet. Shostakovich always attached great importance to the individuality of his four players, as well as to their corporate role within the ensemble, and in these solos he seems privately to greet each musician in turn.

In Quartet no. 15, on the other hand, he simply gives the instruments unusually extended passages to play quite alone. No. 15 has provoked a more varied response than any of his last works save for the corresponding Symphony. But the Quartet is far from quirky, as parts of the Symphony undoubtedly (and intentionally) appear to be, unless its superficially (and intentionally) monotonous tone could be described as such. Its six *Adagios* together last almost forty minutes and initially gave rise to images of a composer spent out, devoid of ideas, inspiration and energy, although even those who found it tedious could hardly fail to acknowledge the unearthly beauty of such passages as the opening *fugato*. It has since been received with rapture, awe and reverence. Certainly no. 15 requires especially attentive listening, so that, as the first movement begins to unfold, one is hypnotised into the extended time scale. The extraordinary variety achieved within one tempo designation is then revealed to the full. The metronome marking of '♩ = 80' changes only for the funeral march and sections of the epilogue, and then it is to the still slower '♩ = 60'. Emotionally, there is little to relieve the all-pervading gloom and yet it is far removed from the desperate agony of no. 13. Instead there is a feeling of calm, of serenity. When the Fitzwilliam first played the work in the former USSR immediately after the composer's death, we were informed, on more than one occasion, that he had been deliberately composing his own requiem.

There has been some confusion over the dedication of no. 15. It was thought to have been written in memory of the cellist Shirinsky (which it may well have been) and the first major catalogue of Shostakovich's works seemed to confirm this. But there is no mention of this dedication in the score, and in a letter dated 28 March 1975, Dmitri Dmitrievich [Shostakovich] told me quite categorically that it was dedicated to no-one. By now he really was communing only with himself. Shostakovich was a composer who thrived on direct emotional contact with his listeners (and with his players also) and in this last quartet, the emotional response is achieved by drawing us ever more deeply into his private world. The final pages recall blurred memories of earlier parts of the work, amid a weird succession of rustlings, tappings, wailings, and shudderings. Instrumental colour is exploited in a highly original way, giving a truly eerie, almost supernatural effect that was likened by a Latvian writer friend to "the howling of the wind in the cemetery".[7] The semitone trill is an ever-present spectre, as it often is in these final compositions, and one might speculate on its significance as a symbol of the death obsession which continually haunted this stricken man during his last years. At the end it leads the way to the final chant, through it and beyond it into nothingness. Shostakovich takes leave of the string quartet in a state of resignation and acceptance.

[7] Muske, Via. Review of a concert in Riga by the Fitzwilliam Quartet, 11 November 1976.

V
The British Quartet

Anthony Gilbert

It should first be said that I present this broad survey not as a musicologist, a historian or a social commentator, but as a composer. This is likely to give my words a composer's bias and prejudices, but it also gives them, I hope, just a bit of composer's insight – the insight of one who has known personally all but the first of the seventeen quartet composers touched upon, who has worked closely with about half of them, and who has known many of them as close personal friends. So what follows comes from the heart. The views are likely to be intensely personal, even unorthodox, and the choice of works likewise. Consequently, there are many significant (as well as insignificant) omissions in what follows.[1] What I have tried to do is to concentrate on quartets in which the composer has extended the boundaries of musical experience, speaking to me of things which can be spoken of in no other way. Words like 'vision' or 'spirituality' only convey part of what I am trying to describe. To those composers who feel unjustly neglected, I simply apologise and point out that my own quartets have likewise been left undealt-with herein.

THE ENGLISH TRADITION ENCOUNTERS NEW EUROPEAN INFLUENCES

Unlike Russia or the United States or Australia, where the medium tends to be dominated by the works of individual composers, in twentieth-century Britain there have been well over a score of composers of outstanding string quartets. So to provide some sort of limitation, my starting point has been determined by when the century began for me – in the mid-1930s. Taking the broader view, this proves a less arbitrary and more meaningful approach

---

[1] Since this article was originally prepared as an illustrated lecture presented as part of the RNCM's QuartetFest 2000, I excluded some of the works that were, in any case, to be heard and spoken about in the Festival. Others were omitted for purely practical reasons: it was, for example, impossible to include a shortish extract from John Tavener's String Quartet *The Hidden Treasure* since its impact depends predominantly on its slow, dreamlike unfolding.

than one might normally expect.

What sort of medium is the string quartet? We might all agree that it is the one in which composers express the essence of themselves at that particular juncture in their lives, so by the same token one might hope that a group of string quartets from any given historical period would express the true underlying spirit of that period. As a medium it is private, intimate, intensely expressive, subtle and detailed, but not highly coloured. The quartet's capacity for precise shading parallels those wonderful early black-and-white portrait photographs one still sees, or the superb photojournalism of the old *Picture Post* magazine.

And in a sense, the quartet is just such a photographic medium. The Fourth Quartet of Frank Bridge (1879-1941), for example, tells us a lot, in black-and-white, about the composer – his breadth of outlook, contemporary concerns, passion (his unexpected passion, when you consider the persona portrayed in the Britten biographies – homely, testy, tennis-playing, above all avuncular); it shows too his intellectual rigour, with sparing use of motifs, a logical and audible connection between material types and careful use of harmonic tension. And further it reflects his musical concerns. Remember that Alban Berg, whose influence is felt so clearly in key passages of this quartet, was a member of the Second Viennese School, and that Vienna at that time was being brought under the Nazi yoke. I owe the moment of my own birth to the shock of Chancellor Dollfuss's assassination, and it is very possible that Bridge's Fourth Quartet, completed in 1937, was shocked into being in the same way. Frank Bridge was the father, and not the uncle, of the twentieth-century British string quartet. He, even more than Elgar or Delius, was the composer who set the tone for the genre – technically, emotionally, and in the way that he made his quartets the focal point of his *œuvre*, representing its essence at whatever point in his life they were written.

It was under the guidance of Bridge that Benjamin Britten wrote his first proper quartet, the *Quartettino* of 1930. He went on to write four more, if you count the *Phantasy Quartet*, each representing the nub of his musical preoccupations, even his musical personality, at the time.

Britten was born in 1913 (again, a traumatic time in our history), and died sixty-three years later, at a time when public appreciation of his work was *just* on the wane, just past its most in-

tense point – a fact Britten himself was aware of, and deeply sensitive to. Listeners' ears were becoming increasingly attuned to the
voice of the visionary Tippett whose messages were more suited to
the cultural climate of the 1970s. Britten's sense of increasing isolation comes across in his Third Quartet, written at a time when
he also knew perfectly well that he was dying. It contains an intensely moving *Passacaglia*, from which significant comparisons can
be drawn with the closing *Chacony* of the Second Quartet. This
latter is a work showing the much more positive side of Britten's
musical character, and was written, interestingly, in 1945. On listening to this forceful movement, several features will immediately be apparent in contrast to the Bridge Fourth Quartet: leaner,
cleaner textures, a certain classical detachment, and a big step
back in harmonic and linear terms to a more diatonic, more consonant language.

It would be wrong to infer from this that Britten was a reactionary in relation to Bridge, turning away from the Viennese influence in favour of a safer tradition. Bridge had wanted him to have
the chance of postgraduate study with Alban Berg, echoes of whose
idiom are clearly evident in that early *Quartettino*. The young Britten
had been devastated by his parents' decision, influenced by his
official teacher John Ireland, not to let him go. Their refusal haunted
him for a lot of his lifetime. But by 1945 he had well and truly
discovered his mature idiom, knew precisely where it had its origins – in the strength and simplicity and pure structural principles
of Henry Purcell – and was prepared to give public acknowledge-
ment of that debt, specifically in the *Chacony* which was written in
the two hundred and fiftieth anniversary year of Purcell's death.
This was not pastiche, or an early form of post-modernism, but
straightforward reinterpretation of sound pre-classical principles.
Compared with several of his contemporaries, Britten did not write
much chamber music, but the little he did produce is outstanding
in its own right, and also, interestingly, very different in its level of
technical concentration and intensity from most of his other work.
The chamber music, perhaps even more than the songs, is the
essential Britten.

The same can be said of his slightly older contemporary, Michael
Tippett (1905-1998). Not counting two earlier works that have
been kept under wraps, Tippett wrote five quartets. They were
spread over the greater part of his composing life. Each one ap-

peared at a crucial time, usually just before a slight but significant stylistic or technical shift as though it were some kind of summation of where he stood, technically and idiomatically, with feelers put out towards the new direction. In these five works, the references beyond the actual music are not socio-political as they are in his operas and cantatas or in, say, the quartets of Shostakovich, but are absolutely and intrinsically musical. The later quartets take Beethoven as their starting-point, but the earlier ones grow out of the English madrigal. For Tippett, the madrigal was not an out-dated genre, as his 1942 madrigal setting of Gerard Manley Hopkins's *The Windhover* proves. Indeed he drew his techniques not only from the madrigalists but also specifically from the poetry of Hopkins. This gifted and many-sided Jesuit was himself a notably musical poet – he even made his own settings of poems of contemporaries such as Coventry Patmore. But for all his composerly gifts, the most progressive musical ideas were to be found in Hopkins's poetry itself, in his use of techniques such as assonance, a way of choosing combinations of words with matching patterns of vowel sounds and reinterpreting these as patterns of recurring harmonic colours – as in

" I caught this morning morning's minion, king-
    dom of daylight's dauphin, dapple-dawn-drawn Falcon,
                                in his riding…",

the opening lines of *The Windhover* – or sprung rhythm, a play of accents more common in song than in poesy, which you can hear in the same passage. Derivatives of these devices, such as additive rhythm and harmonic motifs, are found everywhere in, for example, Stravinsky or Messiaen, and are used compellingly in the Scherzo movement of Tippett's Second Quartet, a work written, significantly, in the same year as his setting of *The Windhover*.

   The third in this group of composers little affected either by the conservatism of Elgar or by the ultra-progressiveness of the Second Viennese School was Elizabeth Maconchy, who was born in 1907, two years later than Tippett, and died in 1994. Maconchy was Irish, but moved to England in her late teens to study at the Royal College of Music. Following this (despite the College Principal's view that she should get married and stay at home), she took her teacher Vaughan Williams's advice and travelled to Prague for postgraduate study with the progressive composer Karel Jirák, an active participant in the affairs of the International Society for

Contemporary Music. Maconchy's contribution to the quartet medium is quite simply that of a colossus among twentieth-century composers: thirteen works, and what she has to say in them is full of personal intensity, passion and vigour. She was as vigorous in her own life, overcoming severe tuberculosis to rear a family, playing a leading role in the promotion of new music in Britain and continuing to work and to supervise recordings of her quartets right up to the last year of her life. If I needed a powerful single example of a quartet which presented essential truths about its composer, I could choose practically any of the Maconchy's; the fourth movement of her Fifth Quartet, written in 1948 when she was at the height of her powers, is as characteristic an example as any. In this can be heard clear Eastern European undertones, with driving rhythms perhaps more Bartókian than Czech. There is also, in the turns of melodic phrase, a hint of Irish folk melody; above all, the music has an unstoppable energy which goes far beyond the bounds of this short movement. This is timeless music, uncluttered by fashionable stylistic baggage.

The 'Avant-garde' Element, and a Consequence

British composers between the wars did not have ready access to the music of the Second Viennese School. Not that it was unobtainable – we did not experience Russia's politically-motivated isolation from avant-garde influences. In Britain we were just rather insular where music was concerned, and I dare say intellectually rather lazy too – then, as now, perhaps?

It needed a non-conformist like Elisabeth Lutyens (1906-1983) to look out and beyond. Lutyens had been exposed to external influences all her life. Her father was an internationally-known architect, and her mother, descended from aristocrats with international connections, hauled her half-way round the world in her pursuit of Madame Blavatsky and Theosophy. Like Elizabeth Maconchy, she fought a successful battle with tuberculosis; she also fought an only marginally less successful one with alcoholism, though neither of these afflictions in any way affected her colossal capacity for work. Her second husband, Edward Clark, was deeply involved with the International Society for Contemporary Music and also unpaid New Music Advisor to the BBC, so she was able to travel to the international festivals and hear what was what in the West. The 'English' style bored her – she has been credited with a number of trenchant aphorisms at its expense. That of Webern, on the other hand, with its purity, clarity and logic, excited her. She heard passion in these tersely expressive short lines, wide intervals and unsettling rhythms, and in her thirteen string quartets in particular, she was able to reflect and develop in her own highly personal way all these characteristics, thereby giving the music a wonderful symmetry of architecture. The palindrome, straight or varied, is one of her structural hallmarks. One might take as an example the first movement of her Sixth Quartet, one of three written in 1952. It has beautifully balanced phrases, sonorous textures, and a way of writing for strings that, while not markedly different in its textural or gestural quality from most of her other work, remains wholly idiomatic. Elisabeth Lutyens was the consummate professional in her approach to the medium, and also the complete individualist. In the 1960s, it was the general, unkind perception among the succeeding generation of composers that, whoever, was leading the way, you could be sure to find Liz following right behind them. Nothing could be further from the truth. One has only to observe the amazing consistency of the main output of her mature years, and the originality of the best of it, to see that Lutyens was pursuing entirely her own path.

Fortunately, we in Britain could not isolate ourselves from continental influences for ever, and one of the most powerful forces for change, certainly with regard to the development of a more 'international' idiom in Britain, was that of Hungarian teacher and composer Mátyás Seiber (1905-1960). As a Jew Seiber knew all about the dangers of a nationalistic culture, and was in his quiet way horrified by the symptoms of it that he found in the British music that people were listening to. (The 'Land of Hope and Glory' club still has an eager membership, as well as its baby fin-de-siècle granddaughter, the 'Cool Britannia' movement.) Seiber had studied with Kodály who was penalised by the authorities for failing to suppress this particular student's progressive, outward-looking tendencies. As an 'escape', Seiber moved to Frankfurt where he joined the staff of the Hoch Conservatory. There, since he wasn't allowed to teach serial techniques, he taught jazz. On Hitler's accession as Chancellor, Seiber moved to London, was interned at the outbreak of war as citizen of a hostile nation, and on his release returned to teaching at Morley College alongside Michael Tippett and the conductor Walter Goehr, a former Schoenberg pupil –

radicals all. Seiber also took as private pupils students from two generations of younger British composers, among them Anthony Milner, Hugh Wood and myself. Along with another fugitive from Nazism, the Romanian Francis Chagrin, he founded the Society for the Promotion of New Music, which is still the principal body in Britain giving young composers a first footing in the profession. Seiber's Third Quartet, the beautiful, Berg-influenced *Quartetto Lirico*, is all-too seldom played. It is a crystalline example of his mature idiom.

During the period of Britain's cultural recovery from the effects of war, the best-known of Seiber's pupils was Peter Racine Fricker. Fricker was born in 1920, and so was nineteen when the Second World War broke out. His musical studies therefore had to be set aside until he had completed his war service. In the ensuing few years he quickly made up for lost time, gaining many major international awards, commissions and premieres before his mid-thirties. Fricker had a natural instinct for cohesive forms and self-determining structures, an individual, dark-toned harmonic language and a great gift for clear contrapuntal writing. The Second Quartet, one of his first really mature works, is characteristic: a deeply personal statement, sombre and compelling but totally unrhetorical. We should hear more of this music. Fricker's is one of the really powerful voices of the immediate post-war years – the voice of one who, like Siegfried Sassoon two generations before, had experienced war in the field. Peter Racine Fricker died in 1990. His following among the young in the 1950s was extraordinarily spontaneous – not at all like the media-generated flavour-of-the-year type of consciousness that audiences seem to be victims of now. It was possible to go to a packed concert with a work of Stravinsky in it and find oneself chatting to as many Fricker fans as Stravinsky ones – young people who were prepared to discourse passionately on the comparative virtues of Fricker and his now-nearly-forgotten contemporary, the late Iain Hamilton.

Nonetheless, within fifteen years Fricker's star was no longer in the ascendant. By 1960 the dark years were forgotten, and young *aficionados of* new music wanted spicier fare. Their attention began to be drawn by a new and charismatic generation of anarchic composers, all born in 1932 or 1934 and fortunately all still with us. These young people were prepared to cut themselves off for the time being from their British roots, for all their admiration for Britten and Tippett, and become fully-paid-up members of the European avant-garde, not mere reflections of it. They maintained high profiles at Darmstadt and the international festivals, and their works received as many performances abroad as at home – if not more. And significantly, for the first time since the war, these composers pursued their main studies overseas.

Peter Maxwell Davies, who was born in Salford in 1934, studied in Italy with Petrassi and through him gained a very special insight into the music of Claudio Monteverdi, with the result that on returning, during his years as a high-profile music master at Cirencester Grammar School, he wrote a triptych of works inspired by the *Vespers* of 1610. The most concentrated of these was his First Quartet, many of whose structural and textural procedures were drawn directly from the Monteverdi – procedures entirely revolutionary in quartet writing but central to Maxwell Davies's own development as a composer at the time. Thus, for example, the way the second half of this quartet is structured on a rotating central *cantus firmus* (in Maxwell Davies's case varied on each new rotation) parallels the *Sonata sopra Sancta Maria* in the Monteverdi wherein the *Sancta Maria* plainchant is constantly repeated with different instrumental elaboration on each appearance. The first movement of the Quartet is like a skeletal version of this, in which the simple chant-line, an octave-displaced version of the composer's own Marian carol melody 'Ave Maria, Hail Blessed Flower' (in the original full score this *cantus* was printed in red) sprouts its own slow five-note elaborations, phrase by phrase, united by a motivic minor third. Maxwell Davies called this quartet an 'apprentice' work, but there are notable historical instances of apprentices producing masterworks, and very possibly this is one such.

The First Quartet is dedicated to Alexander Goehr, Maxwell Davies's contemporary at the Royal Manchester College of Music, who I suspect had a powerful influence on his early development. Goehr, the son of Walter Goehr, was born in Berlin in 1932, two years before Maxwell Davies, escaping with his family to England in early childhood. It is fair to say that Goehr's consciousness has always been far more European than British. Thus, the first of Goehr's four quartets is an interesting, intense, rather Schoenbergian composition. Written just after his studies in Paris with Messiaen and Yvonne Loriod, it might also be called an apprentice work – a

view that seems to be supported by the fact that he fairly extensively revised it thirty years later. By the time Goehr came to write
his Third Quartet in 1976, however, the Schoenbergian influence
he had absorbed through detailed early study, and the influence of
Messiaen similarly absorbed a little later, had become fully assimi-
lated into an incisively elegant personal language, refined in the
course of several other striking chamber compositions that he had
produced in the intervening years: a Suite for the Melos Ensemble,
a Second Quartet, a Piano Trio for Yehudi and Hephzibah Menuhin
and Maurice Gendron, and a Wind Octet. The Third Quartet is
still a serial work, in Goehr's way of being serial – in fact Tony
Burton in his sleeve note to the Lindsay Quartet's recording calls
this the last of Goehr's serial works (though how he can be sure of
that is not clear). What is clear, however, is that the language is
not atonal (in fact the whole work ends with what sounds danger-
ously like a perfect cadence) and that the harmonies and pitch
relationships have a highly individual delicacy and piquancy. Lin-
guistically this could be called a threshold work, a work on the
edge of serialism looking outward to what Goehr described to me
at the time as a simpler language based on common musical prop-
erty. The scherzo-like movement in that Third Quartet has him
exploring texture (the hocketing, *pizzicato*-like patterns, for instance), with contrasted block structures and a dance-like phrase-
ology. It has a curiously elastic tempo, with sudden irruptions of
densely-textured ferocity, and a tremendous sense of pace. Comparison of his four quartets shows Alexander Goehr to be an intensely self-questioning composer, whose idiom and approaches
to composition are fluid, shifting and in a constant state of self-
renewal.

Hugh Wood (b. 1932), Alexander Goehr's long-standing friend
and exact contemporary, was also, until their retirement in July
1999, his colleague on the Music Faculty at Cambridge where
Goehr was professor. If Goehr had his roots in Schoenberg, it is
arguable that Wood's lay in Berg, with an awareness of that music
inevitably sharpened by a consciousness of post-war European
avant-garde techniques. And Berg-like, his music has now opened
itself up to more popular, even populist influences, as his recent
Piano Concerto showed – a work written for, and possibly influenced by, Joanna MacGregor, who had been a student of his at
Cambridge. Hugh Wood has written three quartets, each one log-

ging a phase in the development of his powerful personal voice. When I first heard the Second, at the 1971 ISCM World Music Days, I found it riveting in its clarity, vigour and gritty integrity, and was overwhelmed by the inexorable force of such developmental processes as the build-up towards the climax of its first section. Wood was for a while a Seiber pupil, and this quartet is clear evidence of his readiness to absorb and reinterpret Seiber's urgent messages concerning the power of structural logic.

Throughout most of the 1960s, Wood and Goehr lived as near-neighbours just south of the Thames at Barnes. The Goehr household in particular formed a welcoming focus for much of the significant young composing talent of the time, and also for many of the young performers then eager to accept the challenge of contemporary music. A couple of miles down-river lived Nicholas Maw, until aircraft noise and impaired health drove him to seek out the peace and clean air of the West Country. Maw, who was born in 1935, went to Paris on graduating, ostensibly to study with Nadia Boulanger. Finding her teaching methods and his co-students uncongenial, however, he sought out the Austrian-born composer Max Deutsch as mentor. Deutsch, then in his sixties, was a Schoenbergian. His analytical approach to teaching was unusually stimulating and had an intellectual integrity that chimed in much more readily with Maw's needs as a developing young composer. He returned to England keyed up to take his place among the young avant-garde, but after writing only two works in a progressive idiom, he lost conviction and, as far as the outside world was concerned, stopped composing altogether. In reality he was undergoing a total change of direction. Maw was reinventing himself as a neo-romantic on a grand scale, and from then on would only write works of uncommon length and grandeur. This, as only a composer who has lived through the doctrinaire 1950s and '60s can know, took tremendous courage. The first of his three string quartets was commissioned for the Alberni String Quartet, then quartet-in-residence at Harlow New Town. It emerged as a forty-minute work: the longest single movement for string quartet to have been written at that time. The language is typical of Maw of the period: rich and sensuous, with powerful climaxes and long, elaborate lines, showing a musical imagination of compelling power, worlds away from the pat neo-Romanticism fashionable in the succeeding decades.

THE NEW COMPLEXITY

Inevitably, modernism in Britain began in the 1960s to move into a whole new phase. At about the time the Maw Quartet received its first performance in 1965, the twenty-two-year-old Brian Ferneyhough began postgraduate studies with Maw's first teacher, Lennox Berkeley, at the Royal Academy of Music. Berkeley was a remarkable teacher, seemingly having complete sympathy with students light years away from him in style and ethos – none more so than Ferneyhough, the culmination of whose study period was a very large composition for string quartet with the title *Sonatas*. This work in fact consisted of twenty-four short string Fantasias to be played as an interrupted continuum of some fifty minutes' duration. It was written (almost incredibly, considering the extreme complexity of the music) between August and December of 1967. *Sonatas*, like all Ferneyhough's music that followed, is characterised by an extraordinary intensity of expression, an extension of the techniques of string playing beyond virtually anything else attempted at that time, and an almost ferocious concentration on detail. As one might imagine, given these qualities, it is seldom played: indeed, despite determined attempts by well-wishers in England in the two years following its completion, the work was not performed in full until 1976, at the Royan Festival, where it immediately placed Ferneyhough in the forefront of the European avant-garde. In the meantime, Ferneyhough had become somewhat disillusioned with the British contemporary scene, and had moved to Europe for further study, notably with Klaus Huber in Basel. He followed Huber to Freiburg, where he himself became something of a guru until moving to the United States a few years ago. Brian Ferneyhough has written three further string quartets, of which, because it is my own favourite, I particularly recommend the Second of 1980, which typifies Ferneyhough's so-called 'mannerist' style and technique: the clear, if somewhat idiosyncratic formal logic and the intensely rich detail of the foreground: fragmented, microtonal on occasion, always with particular attention in the score to sound quality and details of phrasing and dynamics.

Michael Finnissy, born in 1936 and therefore three years younger than Ferneyhough, has often been bracketed with him and, together, they are regarded as leaders of the so-called 'New Complexity' movement in Europe. Finnissy's output is huge, and is in fact by no means confined to music of intense complexity. He has a great interest in folk music and in music of other cultures, and is as perfectly capable of writing partsongs of the utmost simplicity for amateur choir as he is of writing music of extreme virtuosity for his own instrument, the piano. Like Ferneyhough, Finnissy passionately believes that listening should not be a mere passive state but an act requiring considerable intellectual effort and even stamina. He pays his listeners the compliment of treating them as equals, in the firm belief that such a stimulus, such an intensity of experience, leaves them permanently if subtly changed, with awarenesses heightened and preconceptions removed. Finnissy's 1984 Quartet is remarkable in its radical approach to the medium. For the first seven minutes of this twenty-two minute work all instruments remain *pianissimo*, high in the treble range, creating an insect-world of almost unbearable tension. All parts are seemingly independent but all are notated with meticulous rhythmic precision, so that no one player runs the risk of straying from the others. To hear how Finnissy handles material of folk origin in the medium, the reader should listen to *Multiple Forms of Constraint*, in which he gives a simple, expressive melody of Bulgarian origin to the first violin, seated separately from the other three players, and allows this material to 'bleed out' to the others where it proliferates, with microtonal inflections and fluid polyphony – characteristics typical of Finnissy's music.

DIVERSIFICATION

Multiple Forms of Constraint illustrates how the tight, rigid, self-enclosed constraints of 'New Complexity' can yield to external influences and indeed by the 1980s diversification, multiplicity and pluralism were the more obvious characteristics of British culture, most particularly in music. In those years no one force predominated – though heaven knows each one tried to. There were plenty of public debates between the advocates of post-modernism, neo-romanticism and the new complexity, and attending a contemporary music festival could be a very exciting, charged experience. All this was fine, but it carried with it the risk of diverting attention from the work of true individualists, those few important voices who remained pretty well unaffected by these posturings, making nevertheless (or perhaps consequently) significant contributions to the diversification process.

For the first of these, it is necessary to step back a generation and look at a major Australian composer who has spent his entire professional life working in England. David Lumsdaine was born in 1931 in Sydney, and came to England at the age of twenty-one to pursue postgraduate studies with our two leading teachers of the time, Mátyás Seiber and Lennox Berkeley. For nearly twenty years Lumsdaine embraced important facets of the European avant-garde and its complex techniques, becoming in the process Britain's most advanced exponent and teacher of serial permutation processes. Then in 1972 he returned for the first time to Australia and rediscovered not so much its contemporary music as its birdsong and its landscapes. His music, in consequence, expanded and became richer and more colourful, and its beneath-the-surface complexity found a fitting context. Lumsdaine's forms and processes had always been dependent upon cycles, and upon the idea of the end being no more than the anticipation of a new beginning. In this regard there is a close connection with the composer's interest in recording birdsong, in pursuit of which he will set up his gear in a remote spot well before dawn, and remain there for hours on end recording the slow changes that take place in the density, intensity and character of the song, the way in which one species gives way to another and the way in which the whole fabric is dependent upon the season, the light and a whole range of other cyclically-changing factors.

Lumsdaine's *Mandala IV* for string quartet is a work typifying this approach. It was long in the making, but reached some sort of definitive form in 1983. There is an extraordinary imagination at work here with strange, haunted visions of a dying land as a background to dancing phrases and gestures of surging vitality. The structure is open – you, the listener, are invited to find your own way through this singing forest. A *mandala*, after all, is an object one meditates upon as a way of at once focusing the mind and opening it up. Time and space become immeasurable, almost interchangeable.

When Nicola LeFanu (b. 1947) first met David Lumsdaine she was a bright young prizewinning composer just a few years on from her studies at Oxford and the Royal College of Music, so a lot of her artistic maturing has really taken place during the twenty-nine years or more of their close association and marriage. As the daughter of Elizabeth Maconchy, she was almost bound to write a string quartet sooner or later – later, as it turned out, for the first of her two quartets was written only in 1988. This has the passion of her mother's work in full measure, and there is in it a touch of its Irish folk lilt and of its dancing. But the language, the sense of space, the informal structure and the feeling of spontaneity owe something to Lumsdaine too. A feature of LeFanu's sensitive, subtle musical language is the use of quarter-tone melodic inflections and curious, tight harmonies formed also from microtonal intervals. Her ear for microtones is peculiarly sensitive. She does not bombard us with them, as do some composers of the 'New Complexity' school, but uses them for purely expressive means, much as, for example, Indian musicians do. The consequence is that the listener quickly perceives the point of their use, and quickly therefore adjusts to the language. Nicola, now Professor of Music at York University, has written of one or two other strong formative influences in her life and in particular of her years as a pre-College student working under the supervision of Jeremy Dale Roberts who, until his retirement in the summer of 1999, was Head of Composition at the Royal College of Music. Jeremy's work both as a teacher and a composer should have placed him in the forefront of British music; alas, for reasons only known to those who control the London musical scene, he has never been allowed to take his rightful place.

In 1988, the year that Nicola LeFanu wrote her First Quartet, Martin Butler wrote his Third. Butler, who was born in 1960 and so is young enough to have studied at the Royal Northern College of Music, first with Petr Eben and then with myself, had the even greater benefit during his later student year of sharing a house with the Brodsky Quartet. What could have been more natural, therefore, than for him to write his first two quartets, the earlier of which has traces of Tippett, for the Brodsky? After leaving Manchester, there was an important year in the 'wilderness', struggling to find a personal idiom, and then a Fulbright Fellowship enabled him to go to Princeton University. Here his principal supervisor was Paul Lansky, who introduced him to the rich possibilities that folk idioms could offer: blue-grass, hoe-down, funky-pop, rhythm 'n' blues and, in the case of the Third Quartet, Irish folk-fiddling. This quartet, called *Songs and Dances from a Haunted Place*, started life in the composer's mind as a piece for solo viola, and indeed it is the viola that gives out the first phrases of the slow fantasy that forms its first half. However, the idea of a ghostly fiddler sitting on a rock in the middle of a deserted moor soon took over, so what we in fact hear are four players being encouraged to sound like one instrument, particularly in the *moto perpetuo* Jig which constitutes the second half of the work.

While on the question of writing techniques for the string quartet medium, it is perhaps worth noting how quickly British composers drew back from the idea of exploring new ways of addressing their players' instruments. Tapping on the belly, bowing on the wrong side of the bridge and amplification all too readily became clichés. Quartets such as the Arditti and the Kronos are well accustomed to all these techniques but there is something in the nature of British composers' perception of the medium that more often than not causes them to hold fast to the essential bowed, undistorted sound. So, leaving aside certain works in the 'New Complexity' idiom, the most radical approach we might find in this area is the odd eccentric wanting to make the quartet sound like a giant hurdy-gurdy[2] or as with the Butler, like a vast echoing folk-fiddle.

Simon Holt, who was born in 1958, was in the same year as Martin Butler at the RNCM, graduating with him in 1982. With his idiom and technique already fully developed, he very quickly found his way in the profession. Moving to London (still a wise thing for a young composer to do), he in due course found himself living a few doors away from Peter Manning, then leader of the Britten Quartet. In the fullness of time, a commission followed and in 1989 he wrote his only quartet so far, a remarkable single-movement work called *Danger of the Disappearance of Things*. The pregnant title quotes the Swiss sculptor Giacometti's description of the risks inherent in working on the highly-refined pieces he is noted for – typically, his 'thin man' bronzes. Simon Holt, who did a foundation course in art before he entered the RNCM, has from his earliest compositions found inspiration in the work of practitioners in parallel art-forms: sculpture evidently, painting and also poetry, particularly that of Lorca. The music of *Danger of the Disappearance of Things* is taut and highly-refined in the Giacometti

---

[2] The reference here is to the author's own Third Quartet 'Super *Hoqueto David*' (1987). [Ed].

manner, and in this quartet, the composer focuses on a single linear idea, starting slow and tense, which he worries along, slowly transforming it by varied repetition, expansion, elaboration, extension and acceleration, re-shaping it attacking it, walking round and round it rather like a sculptor working first on one aspect, then another, of a single multi-faceted form. Nowadays, the process would be called 'morphing'. The result is a single movement of steely strength and tautness, driven by inexorable forces: the epitome of all that is best in Holt's work.

Postscript

It is arguable that the string quartets touched upon in this survey likewise epitomise the best of British music since the mid-'30s in their cohesiveness and in the almost organic logic of their interrelationships – a feature I have been at pains to highlight. But one should not fall into the trap of assuming they typify British music. I have striven to show that the medium is not a hermetic one, but despite the extraordinary success of the RNCM's QuartetFest 2000, it is hard to prove that it is a cardinal medium in our time. During the months spent researching and preparing this survey, I was struck by the small number of live performances and even broadcasts of contemporary British quartets: far more typical of our current climate has been the succession of sizeable new works for voices and orchestra, works which are mostly episodic, text-dependent and stylistically accessible: true descendants of the nobile lineage of Parry and Stanford. Never mind the string quartet, dear reader; the British oratorio is back among us.

Anthony Gilbert is himself the composer of three (to date) distinguished and highly individual contributions to the quartet repertoire. The First Quartet op. 20a (1972) exists in two versions and can be performed either as a separate self-contained string quartet or with the *Little Piano Pieces* op. 20b to form the *String Quartet with Piano Pieces*, in which case the Piano Pieces, which rework the harmonic and thematic material of the Quartet movements, act as glosses or commentaries. (Gilbert himself has likened the relationship between the two works to that between a medieval manuscript and its marginal decorations). Quartets nos. 2 and 3 both date from 1987. Quartet no. 3 ('Super *Hoqueto David*'), the work referred to here, takes the form of an energetic, if not frenetic, commentary on the Machaut double hocket, in which the quartet writing recaptures the raucous sound of the *organistrum*, the monstrous hurdy-gurdy used by the monks of Machaut's time to accompany the singers and to teach polyphony. [Ed.]

VI

The American Quartet

David Nicholls

E pluribus unum – From many, one

The official motto of the United States of America is direct in its meaning and inspiring in its vision: that out of disparateness – of peoples, beliefs, values, ambitions – should come an overreaching unity of aim and purpose. Certainly, the motto is a statement both of demographic fact, and of political intent. The citizens of the United States – from its aboriginal Native American dwellers, through the voluntary and involuntary colonists of the eighteenth century, to the myriad of nineteenth- and twentieth-century immigrants – come from an extremely diverse range of ethnic and geographical backgrounds. Indeed, until quite recently, America was unique in its demographic diversity.[1] In its constitution, meanwhile, America provides for individual liberty insofar as it does not go against the common good, and for a federated system of government in which the fifty states are able to function quasi-autonomously.[2]

In cultural – and especially musical – terms, however, it is less easy to see how the motto translates directly into practice. Clearly, there are many cultures present in the United States – at least as many cultures as there are distinct cultural groups within the society as a whole. But is there any way in which these cultures can both retain their individual identities *and* coalesce to form a single meta-culture? To put it in simple musical terms, while it is easy to identify a plethora of American musics, is it possible to define *an* American music, either in the quartet literature or more gener-

---

[1] In the contemporary global village, many societies – including those of Great Britain – are multi-ethnic and multi-cultural. But until the second half of the twentieth century only Australia even began to match the United States in the range of its immigrant peoples and cultures.

[2] See the Constitution of the United States for further details, noting particularly its preamble: "We the people of the United States, in order to form a more perfect union, establish Justice, insure domestic tranquility, provide for the common defence, promote the general Welfare, and secure the Blessings of Liberty to ourselves and our Posterity, do ordain and establish this Constitution for the United States of America."

ally? The standard literature both helps and hinders us in this: there are many inclusive publications and series – such as *The New Grove Dictionary of American Music*, *The Cambridge History of American Music*, and *New World Records* – that cover the complete spectrum of American musical achievement, from Barber to barbershop, Cage to Cajun, Ruggles to ragtime, and (Harry) Partch to (Dolly) Parton. Yet there have also been many attempts to privilege one kind of American music above all others, as may be construed from the titles of three representative books published between 1972 and 1986. Barbara L. Tischler's *An American Music* (subtitled 'The Search for an American Musical Identity') deals exclusively with art music, principally between the wars; *American Music*, edited by Charles Nanry, and subtitled 'From Storyville to Woodstock', concerns itself with jazz and rock; finally, the more upfront *Southern Music/American Music* by Bill C. Malone, is a regionally-defined survey of folk and popular music.[3] Ultimately, if there *is* one American sound from among the many – an *'unum e pluribus'* – what is it?

If the answer is difficult to divine now, then things were no less confused a century ago. Although the United States had declared itself politically independent in 1776, by the time of its centennial it still to a considerable extent remained culturally – and especially musically – indentured to Europe. In general terms, the popular songs and instrumental pieces of the music hall and parlour were very similar to those of the British Isles, as too were much hymnody and folk music. Art music modelled itself almost exclusively on the Austro-German tradition, its composers invariably considering their education incomplete without a period of study at a European (and before the First World War, usually German) conservatory. By the time Antonín Dvořák arrived in America in 1893 as Director of the National Conservatory of Music in New York, composers belonging to the so-called Second New England

---

[3] Sadie, Stanley and Hitchcock, H. Wiley (eds.), *The New Grove Dictionary of American Music* (London: Macmillan, 1986); Nicholls, David (ed.), *The Cambridge History of American Music* (Cambridge: Cambridge University Press, 1998); Tischler, Barbara L., *An American Music: the Search for an American Musical Identity* (New York: Oxford University Press, 1986); Nanry, Charles (ed.), *American Music – from Storyville to Woodstock* (New Brunswick, NJ: Transaction Books, 1972); Malone, Bill C., *Southern Music/American Music* (Lexington: Kentucky University Press, 1979).

School – including George W. Chadwick and Amy Cheney Beach – had already begun to write in a 'nationalist' style. Interestingly, the principal features of this style in many ways anticipated the final recipe for the creation of an 'American' music suggested by Dvořák himself; however, his first thoughts on the matter raised many hackles. On 21 May 1893, in an interview in the *New York Herald*, Dvořák had opined that

> the future music of this country must be founded upon what are called the negro melodies [...] This must be the real foundation of any serious and original school of composition to be developed in the United States [...] These are the folk songs of America, and your composers must turn to them [...] [4]

Subsequently, Dvořák modified his views, so that by February 1895, speaking in *Harper's New Monthly Magazine*, he felt that "the germs for the best in music lie hidden among all the races that are commingled in this great country;" but by this time it was too late, for the damage had already been done.

Given his position as a leading European composer, Dvořák's views are entirely reasonable: like Grieg and Tchaikovsky (to name but two others), he was able to create genuinely nationalistic music by integrating into the existing musical *lingua franca* of Europe the folk music of his compatriots. Like the majority of European composers of art music at this time, he spoke a common (essentially Austro-German) musical tongue, but with a characteristic and definable regional (or ethnic) accent. What Dvořák failed to appreciate, though, was that American composers of art music – despite their use of a basic musical language very similar to his own – were not united in their view of what an appropriate 'American' accent might be. In a polyglot society such as America's, there existed a plethora of identifiable regional and ethnic accents, all of which might reasonably claim to be 'American' to some extent. To privilege one or two accents above the others was clearly not practicable, and thus there was the potential in his remarks for offence to be caused to almost everyone. Indeed, given the his-

---

[4] The full text of both this interview and Dvořák's later pronouncements on the subject are reproduced in Tibbetts, John C. (ed.), *Dvořák in America, 1892-1895* (Portland, Or.: Amadeus Press, 1993), pp. 355-384.

torical relationships between black and white Americans, the suggestion that mainly Northern whites should appropriate for nationalistic purposes the music of mainly Southern blacks, shows a remarkable lack of sensitivity.

Following Dvořák's initial pronouncements, a number of prominent New England musicians responded in the columns of the *Boston Herald*.[5] Harvard's John Knowles Paine (1839-1906) stated that Dvořák "greatly overestimates the influence that the national melodies and folk-songs have exercised on the higher forms of musical art", while Amy Beach (1867-1944) noted that "the Africans are no more [one might add 'or no less'] native than the Italians, Swedes or Russians". Several respondents, including Paine, seemed somewhat offended by the suggestion that (in Paine's rather embarrassing words) "[the] future [of] American music will rest upon such a shaky foundation as the melodies of a yet largely undeveloped race...". Yet others took the contrary view, largely accepting Dvořák's suggestions: typical examples of works written in the broad spirit of his remarks include Henry Gilbert's *Dance in Place Congo*, Arthur Farwell's *Navaho War Dance* and Beach's 'Gaelic' Symphony.

Somewhat ironically, and adding hugely to the general confusion over what an 'American' music might be, just at the time Dvořák was inciting American art music composers to acts of cultural imperialism, several interrelated genres of popular music (all of which were to some extent intrinsically linked with African American culture) were about to enter the mainstream of American – and subsequently Western – cultural life. The meteoric rise between 1895 and 1925 of ragtime and blues (with their love-child jazz), together with musical theatre and Tin Pan Alley songs, could not have been predicted by Dvořák or anyone else; nor could the extent to which they would be perceived in the public imagination as the only authentic examples of American music. The degree of their ubiquity by the mid-1920s, and their effect on European (let alone American) art music, is easily demonstrated: think of the *Golliwog's Cake Walk*, *La Création du Monde*, *L'Enfant*

---

[5] Extended extracts from the responses, and a commentary on them, are found in Adrienne Fried Block, 'Boston Talks Back to Dvořák' in *Newsletter of the Institute for Studies in American Music*, 18/2, May 1989, pp. 10-11, 15.

et les sortilèges, Die Dreigroschenoper, or Shostakovich's *Taiti Trot*.[6]

Certainly, by the 1930s, a veritable *smorgasbord* of apparently incompatible musics already sought approbation as the authentic voice of America. In terms of attempting to discuss American string quartets in the twentieth century, then, it should be clear that the initial – and overwhelming – impression is inevitably one of plurality rather than unity, confusion rather than concurrence. Moreover, there are many ways in which the cornucopian abundance of these quartets can be sorted into more-or-less convenient (but not necessarily satisfactory) categories for discussion. My own approach in this essay is a simple one: to consider the works and their composers in terms of the degree to which they adhere to the enduring principles of Western tonality, regardless of the particular accent they might adopt in doing so. Accordingly, I would identify three basic categories: *traditional* string quartets, in which tonality is essentially unquestioned as a musico-linguistic tool; *modernist* quartets, in which the remnants of tonality are used as the foundation for new musico-linguistic developments; and *radical* quartets, the musical languages of which are created empirically, with little or no fundamental reference to tonality, either directly or indirectly.

Typical examples of the first, *traditional*, group include the Quartet no. 3 (1885) of George W. Chadwick (1854-1931); the Quartet no. 4 (1953) of Walter Piston (1894-1976); the *Lullaby* (c. 1920) by George Gershwin (1898-1937); the *Two Pieces* (1923/28) of Aaron Copland (1900-90); and the Quartet (1936) by Samuel Barber (1910-81).[7] Of these, the works by Chadwick, Piston and Barber can be considered concurrently, as although they span a period of almost seventy years, they have much in com-

---

[6] *Taiti Trot* is an arrangement of Vincent Youmans's *Tea for Two*, a song originating in the 1923 musical *No, No, Nanette*. Like so many other musicals at this time, *No, No, Nanette* transferred to London only a few months after its American opening; other contemporaneous examples include Sigmund Romberg's *The Desert Song* and George Gershwin's *Lady, Be Good!*

[7] The choice of quartets discussed in the lecture on which this essay is based was partly determined by the American repertoire being performed during the QuartetFest. Of the works discussed here, those by Barber (*Adagio* only), Carter, Ives, Cowell, Cage, Crumb and Glass were heard during the festival. Whether there is any significance in the fact that five of the seven pieces were from the *radical* group is open to debate.

mon. Chadwick and Piston both wrote five quartets and all share with Barber's single essay in the medium a profound respect for the norms of European art music. It would be easy to suggest that this respect had been inculcated through a continental education – Chadwick studied in Leipzig, and Piston with Boulanger in Paris – were it not for the fact that Barber, who is perhaps the most European of the three in sensibility, studied exclusively at the Curtis Institute in Philadelphia. More important is the fact that each set his standards by the norms of the European art music canon, as is clear from the Brahmsian solidity of Chadwick's opening *Allegro di molto*, the intentionally Italian character of Piston's corresponding *Soave*, or the impassioned lyricism of Barber's famous *Adagio*. In short, there is nothing overtly (or even covertly) 'American' here, whether in terms of subject matter, ethnic or regional accent, or otherwise. In complete contrast, both of the works by Copland and Gershwin are superficially 'America' in their differing invocations of popular music – Copland in the jazzy rhythmic asymmetry of the *Rondino* movement, and Gershwin in the bluesy melody and harmony of the *Lullaby*. Perhaps significantly, though, given the rather serious character of the quartet medium, neither of these archetypal American composers – nor their most obvious successor, Leonard Bernstein – wrote a 'conventional' string quartet.

Thus we have to look elsewhere – in the works of the *modernist* camp – for more typical examples of twentieth-century 'American' quartet writing. Indeed, it is possible to argue that one particular (and readily identifiable) strain of musical Americanism is firmly located in the modernists' hard-headed approach to such canonical genres as the symphony and the quartet, as well as in their empathy with the post-tonal music of Schoenberg and his students. The third of the five quartets by William Schuman (1910-92) dates from 1939 and although eschewing atonality, is certainly chromatically tortuous at various points in its first – Introduction and Fugue – movement. Roger Sessions (1896-1985), meanwhile, came to serialism quite late in his career, but did so as a logical consequence of the increasing chromaticism and complexity of his music. The second of his quartets was completed in 1951, before his formal adoption of twelve-note procedures, and is a knotty piece, made more 'strenuous' (to use Sessions's own word) through the requirement that its movement be played without pause.[8] Among Sessions's students was Milton Babbitt; and both in turn taught Donald Martino (b. 1931) in whose solitary Quartet (1983) one finds an exemplary model of the modernist American string quartet. The piece is at once terse yet lyrical, perhaps reflecting Martino's Italian-German parentage.[9] Its multi-section form encompasses extremes of tempo, register, dynamic, and timbre, and the demands it places on its performers are considerable.

In its overall sound, Martino's piece is curiously similar to many other post-war quartets, including the Fifth and most recent (1995) of Elliott Carter (b. 1908). Carter started his compositional career in the Boulangerie, having studied in Paris between 1932 and 1935, and his early works are overt in their Eurocentricism and neo-Classicism. Subsequently, Carter's music – influenced by modernist developments in both Europe and America – became increasingly complex though he avoided the use of serialism *per se*. A turning-point came with the Quartet no. 1, written in 1950-51 in the Arizona desert; Carter has stated that during the composition of the piece, one thought in particular haunted him: "it was that each idea should seek out its opposite. The result was a series of oppositions between high and low, slow and fast, a broad statement and a delicate, subdued sequel."[10] Later quartets by Carter – which between them span the entire period of his compositional maturity – have similarly pursued the quarry of complexity, especially in rhythm and metre: for instance, in the Quartet no. 2 (1959) each instrument acts

> like a character in an opera made up primarily of 'quartets'. The individuals of this group are related to each other in what might be metaphorically termed three forms of responsiveness: discipleship, companionship, and confrontation.[11]

[8] See Olmstead, Andrea, *Conversations with Roger Sessions* (Boston: Northeastern University Press, 1987), p. 74.

[9] Martino's Italian-German parentage is both genetic and musical, as in addition to the 'German' training he received from Sessions and Babbitt, he also studied with Luigi Dallapiccola.

[10] *Elliott Carter: In Conversation with Enzo Restagno for Settembre Musica 1989* (trans. Katherine Siberblatt Wolfthal). I.S.A.M. Monograph no. 32, (Brooklyn, New York: Institute for Studies in American Music, 1991), p. 53.

[11] Carter's description of the work is quoted in Hitchcock, H. Wiley, *Music in the United States: A Historical Introduction*, 3rd edition, (Englewood Cliffs, NJ: Prentice Hall, 1988), p. 250.

The Quartet no. 5 (1995), a product of Carter's remarkable 'Indian summer', is rather more relaxed than any of its predecessors; however, it still keeps its performers fully occupied, not least in its arresting use of harmonics.

As I noted earlier, there are numerous ways in which one might categorise twentieth-century American music. The threefold division adopted in this essay is generally convenient, but in teasing out the differences between modernism and radicalism is not always entirely successful. The six representative quartets from the *radical* group discussed here are the Quartet no. 2 (1911-13) by Charles Ives (1874-1954), the Quartet no. 4 (1936) by Henry Cowell (1897-1965), the solitary Quartet (1931) of Ruth Crawford Seeger (1901-53), *Thirty Pieces for String Quartet* (1983) by John Cage (1912-92), *Black Angels* (1970) by George Crumb (b. 1929), and the Quartet no. 2 'Company' (1983) by Philip Glass (b. 1937). In general terms, I have no hesitation in placing all of these works in the radical camp, as each has an individual musical language created empirically. However, with the notable exception of the Cage piece, there are aspects of each work that suggest links with the past and/or the tonal present, as will be clear from the following discussion.

At a superficial level, Ives's Quartet no. 2 appears to have little in common with European tradition. The composer described it as a "S.Q. for 4 men – who converse, discuss, argue (in re 'Politick'), fight, shake hands, shut up – then walk up the mountain side to view the firmament!"[12] The tripartite structure of the piece reflects this programme: the first (mainly slow) movement is titled 'Discussions', the (fast) second movement 'Arguments', and the slow finale 'The Call of the Mountains'. The pitch and rhythmic content of the quartet are generally dissonant, and even the shimmering, ecstatic, closing pages are broadly consonant rather than strictly tonal. However, as J. Peter Burkholder has pointed out, the piece (like many others by Ives)

> use[s] quotations [of identifiable tonal melodies] in a symbolic sense [... there are] quick bursts of borrowed fragments to suggest rapid-fire conversation, and *Bethany* and *Westminster Chimes* to evoke

---

[12] Note on the manuscript, quoted in Sinclair, James B., *A Descriptive Catalogue of the Music of Charles Ives* (New Haven, CT: Yale University Press, 1999), p. 143.

the majesty and wonder of contemplating the heavens.[13]

Thus even in a largely self-referential context, Ives alludes to the music of everyday life. Quotation and allusion also characterise George Crumb's *Black Angels*. The overall impression created by the work is one of extreme modernity: the instruments are amplified, make use of 'extended' performance techniques, and are augmented through the employment of maracas, tam-tams, and bowed water-tuned crystal goblets. Crumb explores extremes of pitch, rhythm, timbre and notation, while the work's structure is largely based in numerology. However, for programmatic and related reasons,

> there are several allusions to tonal music in *Black Angels*: a quotation from Schubert's 'Death and the Maiden' quartet [...]; an original *Sarabanda*, which is stylistically synthetic; the sustained B-major tonality of *God-Music*; and several references to the Latin sequence *Dies Irae* [...] The work [also] abounds in conventional musical symbolism such as the *Diabolus in Musica* (the interval of the tritone) and the *Trillo Di Diavolo* (the 'Devil's trill', after Tartini).[14]

In the case of Philip Glass's 'Company', the multiple repetitions so characteristic of minimalism fail to conceal the fact that the material being repeated is extremely consonant. At the other end of the compositional spectrum, Ruth Crawford's Quartet is a prime example of the diaphony – 'sounding apart' – advocated by her teacher, Charles Seeger: the work's four movements are dissonant in both rhythm and pitch, and the third features an eerily pulsating canon of dynamics. Yet in several respects, the Quartet reveals Crawford's intimate knowledge of, and respect for, the music of Schoenberg and Berg. It is only in John Cage's *Thirty Pieces*, then, that we find an unreservedly radical outlook. Indeed, in its extreme diaphony – both literal and metaphorical – the quartet suggests stronger links with Charles Seeger's theory of complete heterophony than with the serialism of Cage's teacher Schoenberg. There is no score for the piece: rather, each of the players is provided with a part containing a series of thirty musical fragments,

---

[13] Burkholder, J. Peter, *All Made of Tunes: Charles Ives and the Uses of Musical Borrowing* (New Haven, CT: Yale University Press, 1995), p. 360.

[14] Gillespie, Don (compiler and ed.), *George Crumb: Profile of a Composer* (New York: C. F. Peters Corporation, 1986), p. 107.

unrelated to each other either successively or simultaneously except through the recurrence of various 'types' of material. The
only general co-ordination between the parts lies in the provision
for each fragment of a start-time-frame and end-time-frame: thus
for fragment 1, each player may commence her/his music at any
time between 0'00" and 0'45", and must finish at some point between 0'30" and 1'15".

I have deliberately left until last the discussion of Henry Cowell's
Quartet no. 4, usually known as the *United Quartet*. This piece is,
on the surface, disarmingly simple: its five movements consist in
the main of melody-and-accompaniment; its rhythms are plain, its
pitches (both horizontally and vertically) consonant; and with a
single exception it springs no timbral surprises either. How can
this quartet even remotely be considered as radical? The answer
lies in Cowell's intention that the piece be

> an attempt toward a more universal musical style [... whose]
> simplicity is drawn from the whole world, instead of from the
> European tradition or any other single tradition [...] There are in it
> elements suggested from every place and period.[15]

Thus in the fourth movement, a dance-like *Allegretto*, there are
melodies and counter-melodies based on two-, three-, four-, five-,
and six-note scales, all of which are presented against drones on
either C or G. The drones and counter-melodies are at any given
moment invariably combined on one instrument, counterpointed
against the principal melody to create characteristic accompani-
ments; the remaining players perform a quasi-colotomic function
in providing a rhythmic background, tapped out on the backs of
their instruments with either the wood of the bow or a padded
drumstick. These rhythmic patterns, like the structure of both the
movement and the work as a whole, are derived from a simple set
of accents. The effect is at once individual yet universal, familiar
yet unfamiliar, conventional yet profoundly radical.[16]

Cowell had arrived at the music of the *United Quartet* via an
unconventional route. Born near San Francisco, as a child he was

---

[15] Cowell, Henry, [introductory notes to the] *United Quartet* (San Francisco: New
Music Edition, 1937), p. [1].
[16] For further, detailed discussion of the *United Quartet*, see Nicholls, David, 'Henry
Cowell's *United Quartet*' in *American Music*, 13/2, Summer 1995, pp. 195-217.

exposed less to Western art music than to Appalachian, Irish, Chinese, Japanese, and Tahitian music. Although during the 1910s and '20s he was a self-styled ultra-modernist, he was also endlessly fascinated by world musics. From the late 1920s he regularly taught courses on 'Music of the World's Peoples' and in 1931 was awarded a Guggenheim Foundation grant to study comparative musicology, Indonesian gamelan, and Carnatic theory, in Berlin. By 1933, when he published the seminal symposium *American Composers on American Music*, Cowell had formed the opinion – fundamentally different from that of Dvořák – that while

> Nationalism in music has no purpose as an aim in itself... Independence [...] is stronger than imitation [... Thus] more national consciousness is a present necessity for American composers [... but] *When this has been accomplished, self-conscious nationalism will no longer be necessary.*[17]

In this, as in so much else, Cowell was the first to take his own advice, though whether he entirely foresaw the result of doing so is a moot point.

In the same year that the symposium was published, Cowell contributed an article to *Modern Music* entitled 'Towards Neo-Primitivism'. In it, he argued that composers should "draw on those materials common to the music of all the peoples of the world, to build a new music particularly related to our own century".[18] Works such as the *United Quartet* show Cowell doing just that, though he was by no means the only American composer of the 1930s to adopt such a stance. For instance, Harry Partch (1901-74) had already, by this time, "tentatively rejected both the intonational system of modern Europe and its concert system".[19] Subsequently, he went on to devise a new and comprehensive intonational system, to build a unique ensemble of instruments capable of per-

---

[17] Cowell, Henry, 'Trends in American Music' in *American Composers on American Music: A Symposium* (ed. Cowell), (New York: Frederick Ungar Publishing Co., 1961 [1933]), p. 13. The emphasis in the final sentence is the author's, rather than Cowell's.
[18] Cowell, Henry, 'Towards Neo-Primitivism' in *Modern Music*, 10/3,1933, p. 151.
[19] Partch, Harry, *Genesis of a Music*, 2nd edition, enlarged, (New York: Da Capo Press, 1979), pp. vi-vii. One might add, not without some irony, that part of Partch's act of rejection was the burning, in a 1930 'auto-da-fé', of his entire compositional output to that point – which included a string quartet written in just intonation dating from around 1925.

forming in that system, and to create an all-embracing aesthetic for his work, which Partch termed 'córporeality'. More recent figures to follow in similar footsteps include Lou Harrrison, Peter Garland, and minimalists La Monte Young and Terry Riley, the last of whom has had a notably productive relationship with the Kronos Quartet.

That Partch, Cowell, and their successors are American composers is unquestionable; but to what extent are works like the *United Quartet* American? Cowell certainly fails to achieve 'Americanness' through any obvious means, such as conforming to American generic stereotypes, the superficial use of 'American' ethnic material, or through association – retrospective or otherwise – with American subject matter. Indeed, the work stands starkly out from all those other 'American' quartets discussed previously, regardless of their very diverse characters, precisely because of its difference and non-conformity. Yet to my mind, a piece like the *United Quartet* is *profoundly* American, for it replicates at a compositional and aesthetic level the unity of aim and purpose enshrined in the nation's motto *'e pluribus unum'* – 'from many, one'. The United States should be deeply proud of music such as this; that it isn't says much about the continuing dominance of American culture and its institutions by outdated Eurocentric attitudes and values – not least as articulated by Dvořák over a century ago – which still equate nationalism with folk music of one sort or another. (In this context, it is worth noting that Gershwin, whose bluesy *Lullaby* was discussed earlier, wrote in *American Composers on American Music* that "jazz I regard as an American folk-music; not the only one, but a very powerful one…"[20]) Radicals such as Cowell, especially in works like the *United Quartet*, are judged – literally and metaphorically – to have failed to wave the American folk music flag either on home territory (wherever that might be) or on territory appropriated from others. Consequently, their profound Americanism has moved them beyond nationalism into conflict with the nation, and has led to their work being shunned by established performers and performance bodies.

---

[20] Gershwin, George, 'The Relation of Jazz to American Music' in Cowell (ed.), *American Composers… op.cit.*, p. 187.

In conclusion, then, I would suggest that while our notion of 'American music' and therefore of the 'American quartet' must of necessity be synonymous with inclusivity and plurality – as befits a national culture constitutionally built on such concepts – this need not necessarily limit its manifestation merely to an infinite variety of self-contained musics, whose only point-in-common is their creation by Americans (Copland, Carter, Cage) usually in America. Rather, as works like Cowell's *United Quartet* demonstrate, it can also define a music so rooted in inclusivity and plurality that it becomes '*unum e pluribus*', universal rather than national, a truly meta-cultural music which – as Cowell suggested in 1933 – can be "particularly related to our own century". That the greatest twentieth-century musical legacy of the most self-consciously nationalistic (yet genuinely multi-ethnic and multi-cultural) country in the world should be a music apparently unacceptable to its own musical establishment is, to say the least, somewhat paradoxical.

VII
The Frontiers of Quartet Technique

Duncan Druce

The violin family, and with it the string quartet, has crossed many frontiers in its long history; literally, in that today's string players come from all over the globe, and the violin has been adopted by many different musical cultures (Cajun music and South Indian classical music are two diverse examples), and metaphorically, in that the violin family and the string quartet have been continually breaking new ground. From the beginning, in the sixteenth century, the violin and its larger family members have been notably versatile – able to play loud or soft, *molto sostenuto* or *prestissimo*, to provide the most incisive articulation and rhythmic lift for dance music, and with the ability to imitate the most varied expression of the human voice. It was this flexibility, this ability to take on the most varied musical tasks, that elevated the violin to its pre-eminent position as a solo instrument in seventeenth-century Italy, and brought the strings, as a group, to the position they still hold today as the backbone of, first, the opera orchestra, then the symphony orchestra.

Already by the 1600s and 1700s, the strings had passed quite a few frontiers. Designed originally as instruments with a range of about two-and-a-half octaves, violinists – then cellists and violists – extended the range further and further upwards. As often happens with novelties, this innovation was not always regarded with favour. Quantz wrote in 1752 complaining of modern Italian violinists that "they seek the greatest beauty at the very place where it is not to be found, to wit, the extremely high register, or at the end of the fingerboard [...] they climb about in the high register like somnambulists on rooftops".[1]

Quite a number of other novelties were introduced in Baroque and Classical times. Some of these once novel ideas, like playing with a mute, on the bridge, using harmonics, and all the different bowing effects that became possible with the Tourte bow (intro-

---

[1] Quantz, Johann Joachim, *Versuch einer Anweisung die Flöte traversiere zu spielen* (Berlin 1752, trans. E. R. Reilly as *On Playing the Flute*, London and New York, 1966), p. 325.

duced at the end of the eighteenth century), have become com-monplace and unremarkable. Others, like the effects obtainable by tuning an instrument differently, have never been established as normal. Mistuning, or *scordatura*, is particularly associated with the great seventeenth-century violinist and composer Biber. An-other great violinist, Paganini, inspired a whole generation of vio-linist and cellist composers during the 1800s to explore the most brilliant-sounding, extreme resources of their instruments. Perhaps the most bizarre nineteenth-century effect was devised by Paganini's French contemporary Pierre Baillot as a way of playing on all four strings at once by unscrewing the bow then reassembling it with the hair, quite slack, *above* the strings and the bow stick passing between the strings and the instrument – a technique that has not become regularly established, probably because of the trouble of doing it.[2]

Baillot was known as a fine quartet player and, by the 1830s when he described that reverse bowing, the string quartet itself had come a long way from its first period in the 1760s and 1770s as essentially domestic players' music to a style designed for the concert hall. Haydn, in the 1790s, pioneered a grander, more dra-matic sort of quartet writing suitable for Salomon's London con-certs, and during the nineteenth century the move to create greater sonority and ever-richer sounds led composers to introduce ex-tensive double stopping and chords, *tremolando* passages and vir-tuoso bowing techniques.

Some writers felt that these developments were contrary to the true, conversational nature of the quartet. Frederick Corder, for example, writing in the first edition of *Grove*, notices in the late Beethoven quartets "how large a compass the four parts are con-stantly made to cover, a space of nearly five octaves sometimes being dashed over, with little care for the poorness and scratchiness of tone thus produced".[3] On the other hand, Corder also casti-gates Mendelssohn for writing quartets that "would sound better if scored for full orchestra", taking as an example the opening of the D major op. 44 Quartet where Mendelssohn has succeeded in

---

[2] Baillot, Pierre, *L'Art du violin: nouvelle méthode* (Paris, 1834, trans. L. Goldberg as *The Art of the Violin*, Evanston, Ill., 1991).

[3] Corder, Frederick, 'Quartet' in Grove, George (ed.), *A Dictionary of Music and Musicians* (London, 1879-89), Vol. 3, p. 58.

producing the most brilliantly resonant sound from the four instruments. For Corder "this is not quartet writing at all", and he concludes sadly that "if the quartet is yet capable of new treatment the second Beethoven, who is to show us fresh marvels, has not yet come".[4]

Corder was certainly not alone in seeking to establish clear boundaries for the quartet. Though the years leading up to 1900 saw an enormous rise of interest in chamber music performance, this was based firmly on the Classical repertoire. The string quartet masterpieces written by, for instance, Brahms, Smetana, Dvořák, Tchaikovsky, Borodin, Verdi, Franck, Debussy – however successful they were individually at extending the quartet's expressive range – did not manage to re-establish the string quartet in the central position that it had held in Viennese Classical times.

For someone writing on this subject in 1900, there would have been plenty of frontiers to describe – technical, formal, expressive, and glimpses of new possibilities beyond them. But I doubt if anyone could have predicted that the string quartet would return to play such a crucial part in twentieth-century music.

There are many reasons why the quartet has returned centre-stage – such as the coincidence of there being many major composers, like Schoenberg, Bartók, Shostakovich, Carter and Tippett, for whom the medium has had particular importance, or the existence of groups able to devote plenty of rehearsal time to demanding new music – but the strings' famous flexibility, and their ability to adapt to any number of different sound-worlds has played an important part in the resurgence. In the early 1900s, the turning away from grand public statements towards more intimate, more psychological concerns also favoured the return to prominence of the quartet. Already, in the years around 1880, Smetana had chosen the medium of the quartet to portray programmatically personal and autobiographical matters, in contrast to the historical, legendary, or landscape subjects of his symphonic poems.

Amongst all the innovations of the twentieth-century quartet, we must make a distinction between those new methods which could just as well be used by other instruments or by voices (the elaborate exploration of simultaneous different tempi in Elliott

---

[4] *Ibid.*

Carter's Third Quartet is a good example), and those techniques peculiar to, or especially apt for, string instruments. It is on this latter category that this study will concentrate. Rather than just providing a catalogue of ground-breaking procedures, I shall instead consider the very different use of novel effects in two works, both written during the last thirty years.

First of all, however, it is important to point out how dramatically the range of string quartet sonorities had expanded in the early years of the last century. In the third of Webern's *Bagatelles* op. 9 (1913), the contrast within the space of a few seconds between *pizzicato* and *arco*, muted and unmuted, harmonics and playing at the bridge, conveys a quite new impression of the sound of the string quartet – fascinating and multi-faceted but expressively extremely radical, leaving behind any standard idea of beautiful sound or conventional idea of musical boundaries, but seeking beauty elsewhere, in a particular, individual pattern of pitches, rhythms and sounds (see Example 1). No less radical is the prominence Bartók gives in his Third Quartet (1927) to the *glissando* which he transforms from an expressive ornament of performance rarely indicated by the composer, to something that is integral, structured even, and with a very different expressive effect. In the same way that ambiguous, complex chromatic harmonies can create instability, these slides seem to tear apart the ordered musical fabric. The expressive *portamento* so beloved of string players (and singers) in the nineteenth century and right up to 1940, would strongly suggest emotions like sadness or passion. These much more disruptive, co-ordinated slides inspire darker, more fearful feelings.

Sliding pitch plays an even more important part in the first of the works I want to consider in more detail – Xenakis's *Tetras* composed in 1983. The title means 'fourness', and the instruments play mostly together, with similar material. There are occasional solo passages, but rarely anything like counterpoint – the nearest we come to this is when slightly different shapes and styles of playing combine to form a single complex texture. The whole work, about fifteen minutes long, is directed to be played without *vibrato* suggesting that what we have come to regard as normal, expressive string playing has no place here. Xenakis asks for quite a number of special effects: an irregular *glissando* formed of small segments of *glissando* interspersed with sustained pitch; noises produced by the

Ex. 1 Third Bagatelle from Webern's
Six Bagatelles op. 9

bow on top of the bridge, on the tail-piece, and by bowing *along* rather than across the lowest string. He also asks for grinding sounds produced by excess pressure on the bow applied near the bridge, percussive sounds with the hand striking the body of the instrument and sounds produced by hitting the strings with either the hair or the wood of the bow. There is also a range of *pizzicato* effects, including a metallic *pizzicato-glissando*, made by stopping the note with the nail of the left-hand finger while a right-hand fingernail slides up or down the string. If Webern had already, in 1913, substantially expanded our ideas of what string sonority might be, Xenakis, alongside others who have used similar effects, has reached a point where any sound can be considered as musical material. When we add to this the density of much of the writing, and the extensive use not only of *glissandi* but of quarter-tones, the result is a piece of extraordinarily fierce intensity (though with passages of extreme delicacy and mystery). Yet this very intensity makes the music extremely compelling, and such is Xenakis's imaginative control of density, speed and of the contrasting sounds and gestures, that one feels oneself drawn along through the whole length of the piece. The arresting quality of the material is complemented by the cogency of the musical argument; as the work progresses we can appreciate how fully and imaginatively each idea is developed.

Music like this depends very largely on its physical impact, which perhaps can only be realised fully in a live performance. Some features in the score show how carefully Xenakis has considered how his music is to be played. Much of the time, he makes use of a semiquaver grid, with the musical events starting or finishing either precisely on the lines of the grid, or spatially situated between the lines. This allows him to give us music that eschews a regular pulse – notated exactly, yet without the need to make complex irrational divisions of the beat. The players are required to play precisely, but can *feel* how their part fits in without having to calculate each detail minutely.

Some of Xenakis's ideas stem directly from playing techniques. At one point there is a loud, fast *glissando* passage, with eventually all four players double stopping. Xenakis writes precise pitches for only one of each pair of notes, but asks the player to keep the two left-hand fingers that are stopping the strings at an equal distance, so the interval between the two notes constantly varies as the fingers move up and down the fingerboard. Normally a player has to struggle to bring musical order from the physical world; here, the particular physical make-up of the instruments is used directly to produce a chaotic sound.

George Crumb's *Black Angels* also includes a great many novel special effects, but used to very different aesthetic ends. The date of completion on the score is 'Friday March 13th 1970 (*in tempore belli*)' and the piece is subtitled '13 Images from the Dark Land'. Crumb was writing at the height of America's involvement in the Vietnam War, and the work's three stages, borrowing from Beethoven's 'Les Adieux' Sonata, are described as 'Departure' (fall from grace), 'Absence' (spiritual annihilation) and 'Return' (redemption). The work is full of symbols (above all the numbers 13 and 7), references – *in tempore belli* (pointing to Haydn's *Mass in the Time of War*, *The Devil's Trill*, *Danse macabre*) – and quotations (from Schubert's 'Death and the Maiden' and from the *Dies Irae* chant).

In musical terms the Xenakis piece, however much it extends the usual sonorous aspect of the quartet, remains every inch a string quartet, whereas the Crumb belongs to a tradition that seeks to use the quartet as a centre for further exploration. In the past this was done by adding instruments to form quintets, sextets and so on. A turning point came, perhaps, with Schoenberg's Second Quartet which, though still a string quartet, needs five performers since a singer joins the ensemble for the last two movements. This certainly subverts the usual idea of the quartet as an abstract, self-sufficient entity; both the presence of the human voice and the precise images provided by the two Stefan George poems that form the text have the effect of providing a strong alternative focus for the music. Schoenberg is evidently concerned to prevent this disruptive influence gaining too much sway. The string players are inevitably heard as an accompaniment some of the time but they continually reassert themselves as a quartet: both vocal movements, for example, begin and end with substantial passages for the instruments alone.

Black Angels needs only the usual four players, so any disruptions come from within. For one thing, the piece is for an *electric* string quartet and the amplification not only allows for a vastly increased dynamic range (Crumb says he wants the loud passages to sound *surreal*, and the opening is as fierce as anything in *Tetras*), but the electric sound itself considerably alters the whole impression the quartet makes, and allows some special effects which might be too quiet in an acoustic performance to make their impact. Thus, Crumb can ask his players to bow not in the normal manner near the bridge, but at the opposite end of the fingerboard, to produce an ethereal, disembodied sound, and also to use a guitar-style 'bottle-neck' technique, with glass rods held in the left hand either striking or sliding along the strings. Crumb asks for quite a few more unusual playing techniques: varying the point of contact of a *col legno battuto* stroke (striking with the wood of the bow) so that it produces a series of different pitches (the principle on which the clavichord works), and using a carefully controlled bow stroke with excess pressure, resulting in a distorted sound an octave below the pitch played. There is also *pizzicato* with a metal plectrum and a thrummed *tremolando* played with thimbles on the fingers, as well as some very original effects with harmonics.

But each player is asked to do a lot more than just play her or his instrument. They have also to emit vocal sounds – shouts, tongue-clicks, whispers (the words are numbers, especially 7 and 13, in many different languages) and each is given an array of 'extra' instruments to use – bowed tam-tams, bowed wine-glasses, and maracas (held in the right hand whilst playing the violin or cello).

These effects, on and away from the instruments, produce a very wide range of sounds that take us, as Xenakis does, a long way from the traditional image of the string quartet. The Xenakis, however, remains intensely concentrated on the sounds of wood, gut and hair, whereas the Crumb is much more divergent. Even though many of the sounds we hear are not string music, the fact that they are performed by the members of the quartet, rather than percussion or vocal specialists, has a powerful integrating effect. Consider the fourth of the thirteen 'images' – 'Devil-music'. This has a wild violin cadenza – the gaunt, sinister silhouette of Paganini is somewhere close at hand – interspersed with sections of the *Dies Irae* played in the grotesque sub-octave manner described. Each of these sections is introduced with a loud tam-tam stroke played by the cellist, so that the hoarse, horrible tone of the second violin and viola seems to grow out of the gong's resonance. This example makes it clear that not only are Crumb's special effects most beautifully and precisely worked out, but that he has also taken care that the notated image of the music is made visually vivid.

Ex. 2 Fourth movement of George Crumb's *Black Angels*:
'Devil-music'

The opposite image to 'Devil-music' is, naturally, 'God-music', the tenth section with amplified cello indicated as 'Vox Dei'. The cello is accompanied by bowed wine-glasses, in three parts, played by the three other instrumentalists; the fact that it is a bowed accompaniment, played by string players, helps to make this into a sort of celestial translation of a string quartet.

Tetras, along with other magnificent works of the latter years of the twentieth century (quartets by Carter, Nono, Ligeti and quite a few others) demonstrates that the string quartet is able constantly to renew itself whilst keeping something of the density of thought, the intimate intensity of expression that are familiar from the great quartets of Beethoven and Schubert, Schoenberg and Bartók. *Black Angels*, however, represents something else; the use of the quartet as a starting-point for the exploration of the evocative qualities of different sounds. This has proved a fruitful course for those composers whose music has a folkloric dimension, including Bartók, of course, and present-day writers such as the South African Kevin Volans. Strings lend themselves to such explorations partly because of the instruments' rich history, their penetration into so many areas of world music, including folk idioms. But even more it is because of their chameleon-like ability to change colour, to imitate or adapt to different demands – the harmonics of the violin, viola and cello, for instance, can easily suggest a wide range of flute sounds. At the same time, the string quartet, wherever it turns up and whatever style it adopts, remains a recognisable group with its own distinctive sound, a symbol of Western music, of forms based on harmony, counterpoint and expressiveness. This is apparent throughout the exceptionally wide range of repertoire recorded by the Kronos Quartet.

Predictions of the future are only valuable as projections of present concerns. However strongly we may feel that, during the latter part of the twentieth century the string quartet reached its ultimate point in both inward exploration and turning outwards to the whole world of music, we would be very rash to imagine the quartet has reached the end of its history and that there will be no new directions and no original departures from anything composed, played and heard up to now.

VIII
The Recorded Legacy

Tully Potter

In this essay, I want to draw attention to recordings of significant quartet ensembles who were closely linked to particular music and particular composers. In doing so, I hope to give some idea of the kind of sound world that the composers themselves would have recognised and, incidentally, to point out the validity of some of the bygone styles of playing. String playing changed a great deal during the twentieth century and many of the gains were accompanied by losses of techniques which suited certain music – especially music of the late Romantic era. Even if we no longer wish to hear techniques such as *portamento* applied to the music, we should reject them by choice rather than through ignorance. But in certain cases such techniques are vitally necessary to the music and it is not always possible to read everything from the printed editions, even when the composers concerned are as careful in marking up their scores as Bartók or Ravel. I shall consider nine composers in chronological order of their dates of birth.

MAX REGER (1873-1916)

The great German composer Max Reger created a unique sound world and had an unsurpassed grasp of musical structure but has been unfairly dismissed by the majority of critics in the English-speaking countries. Most of them know little of his music and when they do come upon any of it, they approach it with grave suspicion. Performances of his music in Britain and America are generally poorly prepared and his reputation therefore becomes mired in a cycle of self-fulfilling prophecies. Yet the more one perseveres with Reger's music, the more one is rewarded. He was, in my opinion, as great a composer as Elgar or Mahler and any quartet ensemble with 'international' pretensions ought to play at least his E flat Quartet op. 109, a masterpiece written in 1909. Any listener who seeks a way into his chamber music should, I suggest, start with the two string trios and this quartet.

Reger collaborated closely with many string players but he had no greater champion than Adolf Busch. Their personal contact began early in 1909 when Bram Eldering, the Dutch quartet leader and violin professor at the Cologne Conservatory, introduced the 17-year-old Busch to Reger with the words: "My pupil here plays your Violin Concerto". "By heart, I suppose," said Reger sarcastically (the work was an hour long and had only recently been premiered and published). "Yes," Busch replied, almost shamefacedly. His elder brother Fritz, who had already mastered the piano reduction of the orchestral accompaniment, was sent for and the resulting performance amazed the composer.[1]

The Busch brothers became part of Reger's intimate circle and his most enthusiastic propagandists. Although Reger died tragically early, so that most of the Busches work on his behalf was done after his death, they had ample opportunity to absorb his idiom at first hand. Adolf, in particular, gave many concerts with Reger himself. The Busch Quartet played all Reger's chamber music for strings and, had its members not boycotted Germany from April 1933 – a high-principled decision which cost them dear– would surely have made the 78 rpm HMV recording of the E flat Quartet. As it was, the project was given to Max Strub's quartet, a splendid group (whose leader, incidentally, was an Eldering pupil and admirer of Busch) but one with no direct link to the composer. Various LP records have since been made, the best being that by the Drolc Quartet, and CDs of the work have been recorded by the Berne, Joachim, Mannheim, Philharmonia and Vogler Quartets.

By the time the Busch Quartet did record op. 109 in 1951, it was almost at the end of its career and its members would probably be horrified to think of us listening to this tape, made in a German radio studio, half a century later. Nevertheless, the performance says much about Adolf Busch's way with Reger and, because of its historic association, should be better known.

From the outset one notices the melodies, which can seem a trifle wishy-washy in the hands of even such a fine ensemble as the Drolc Quartet. Even more than Max Strub, Busch brings out the form of the music, sculpting the outlines which are inherent in the melodies. It is a matter of breathing, phrasing and balancing, not simply taking the shortest distance between two points, and dem-

---

[1] Grüters, Otto, *Adolf Buschs Lebenslauf,* manuscript, Busch Archiv, Max Reger-Institut, Karlsruhe. Cf. Tully Potter, *Adolf Busch: The Life of an Honest Musician* (London: Toccata Press, in preparation).

onstrates that the characteristic Busch *portamento* can have a structural, as well as an expressive, use in helping to bring out the shapes of the phrases. The weight given to each of the four parts is also crucial. The textures become luminous in the Busch performance and one wonders whence comes the idea that Reger wrote thickly-scored, prolix, unintelligible music. The opening movement catches out both the Strub and Drolc groups, who press forward too eagerly, and all the more recent performers take too fast a basic tempo, the Vogler compounding this error by equating louder with faster and quieter with slower, so that the music proceeds in a series of surges. Busch has faith in Reger and knows that the harmonies need space in which to unfold. At the start, he establishes a dream-like atmosphere in just a few bars, and the wistfulness that lies at the heart of op. 109 is brought out in the quieter, slower passages.

The second movement is a superb Scherzo in which Busch's characteristic *staccato* is much in evidence, as well as his geniality. It is taken at a robust tempo, a few imprecisions of ensemble not affecting its air of great good humour. Reger's instructions to the players (almost as prolific as Ravel's in his F major Quartet) become manic in the *Larghetto* and seem to inhibit the Drolc players, although Strub and his colleagues are more assured. Best of all are the Busch foursome, who have thoroughly subsumed all Reger's anxious promptings into their interpretation: from the violins' full G-string tone at the outset, this lovely movement progresses in long-breathed phrases, with every gradation of a full dynamic range observed.

Although Busch and his partners begin the final fugue *con grazia e con spirito* as requested, they pace it so as to make the most of its alternating wit and seriousness. What emerges is a sort of portrait of Reger himself. Every composer deserves to be judged not just by his best work, but through his finest interpreters – and Reger would surely be content to be assessed on this performance alone.

JOSEF SUK (1874-1935)

The Suk recording I would like to recommend next could hardly be more authentic, as the composer himself is playing in the ensemble. Josef Suk was second violinist of the Bohemian or Czech Quartet for forty-one years and wrote many things for himself and his colleagues to play. In the early days he composed in a fresh, melodious style similar to that of his teacher and father-in-law Dvořák, but gradually he became affected by the influences circulating at the turn of the century. The watershed was the Bohemian Quartet's close contact with Max Reǵer, beginning in 1909. Suk's music became steadily more chromatic, although it always remained tonally centred. His B flat Quartet was composed in 1896 in his early manner but gradually he became disenchanted with the *Allegro giocoso* finale and in 1914 rewrote it. By then his style had changed completely and most modern ensembles therefore prefer to play the original finale. But when the Bohemian Quartet came to record the work in 1928, it opted for the revised finale. In this recording you can hear the performing style of the ensemble which is considered the first modern full-time professional quartet. The playing is very much in nineteenth-century mode, with very little *vibrato*, and the gut strings tend to show up any deviation from the true pitch. By 1928, when the recording was made, the group no longer rehearsed with the assiduity of its early years and its precision of ensemble suffered in consequence. But then the Bohemian Quartet was always more interested in the spirit than in the letter of the music and its performances, even on record, displayed an invigorating rhythmic flair. The two violinists, Karel Hoffman and Josef Suk, were the same as at the beginning of the ensemble's career in 1892, but Jiří Herold became the violist in 1906 and Ladislav Zelenka the cellist in 1914. Of course the ensemble's Dvořák recordings were also uniquely authentic, as its original members had known the composer intimately, but sadly it did not record the one work which it premiered, the G major Quartet op. 106.

Arnold Schoenberg (1874-1951)

Of Arnold Schoenberg's four mature quartets, the first two were written for the Rosé Quartet, a splendid but rather old-fashioned ensemble, and the last two for another Viennese group, the Kolisch Quartet. This foursome was famous for having a left-handed leader who sat on the right at the front; it rehearsed from scores and played most of its repertoire by heart.

The story of how the Schoenberg quartets came to be recorded is astonishing. By the mid-1930s, Schoenberg was living in Los Angeles and one of his pupils was the film composer Alfred Newman. The recordings were done as a present from Newman to Schoenberg around New Year 1937 in conjunction with concerts the Kolisch Quartet were giving at UCLA. The rehearsals were held at Schoenberg's home. The project had its limitations: a film recording studio was used and the technicians were not used to recording classical, let alone chamber, music. In the circumstances they did well but the discs were very noisy and, as the few people who had sets were all Schoenberg enthusiasts, the surviving records have been played a good deal, adding wear to the original surface noise.

The Kolisch Quartet is a good example of my contention that if one wants to learn from the way particular musicians play a piece, one needs to know how they play other pieces, so as to filter out their mannerisms and concentrate on purely musical matters. The Kolisch players, with the possible exception of the cellist Benar Heifetz, were not outstanding (and Heifetz, coming from the Russian school with its heavier style of playing, tended to stand out from the others). It is difficult to find good contemporary critiques of their concerts and, taken as a whole, their records are disappointing. If they had not specialised in new music it is, I think, doubtful whether anyone today would have heard of them. Having said all that, they did have their moments, notably a marvellously stylish record of Wolf's *Italian Serenade*, and there is obvious interest in hearing a performance which corresponds to what Schoenberg himself expected to hear. Of particular note is the recording of the Fourth Quartet, which was probably the first performance of the work (we think the world premiere took place the following day but no-one is sure of the date of the recording session). Perhaps the finest movement in the cycle is the *Largo* of the Fourth Quartet with its unison opening, to which the Kolisch players bring tremendous intensity. In fact the whole movement is played with exceptional commitment. Of course the players had to stop every few minutes for the wax master disc to be changed, a handicap which only increases one's admiration for their achievement. As this was a new composition, they did not play by heart, as was their usual practice, but used the printed music.

MAURICE RAVEL (1875-1937)

The score of the Ravel Quartet is peppered with instructions, reflecting the composer's almost obsessive perfectionism. Ravel was very pernickety about how works were to be performed and on a number of occasions he willingly supervised a recording. The result is that we have an unusually rich heritage of 78 rpm records to guide us in reaching an authentic interpretation of the F major

Quartet. First come the two recordings which Ravel himself supervised, one from 1927 by the International Quartet and one from
1934 by the Galimir Quartet. Then there are recordings by the
Léner Quartet which had been coached in the music by the composer, and by four other ensembles whose members were personally acquainted with him: the Quatuors Capet, Calvet, Pro Arte
and Krettly. In the circumstances it may seem strange that I should
recommend the recording with the least accomplished playing but
despite a few technical lapses, it is, I think, the recording that best
represents the composer's wishes.

   In 1927 Ravel's friend André Mangeot, a London-based French
violinist who played a key role in British chamber music, wanted
to record the F major Quartet with his International Quartet. He
had already been one of the earliest performers of both the Piano
Trio and the Sonata for Violin and Cello, so he was well versed in
the Ravel idiom, and the International ensemble had played the
Quartet a good deal. In 1927 they made the very first recording of
the Quartet but they were not happy and got permission to do it
again. Still they were dissatisfied. Ravel, who visited London at
the time, agreed to listen to the recording:

> He consented to hear the records that we had made and he heard
> them in a little cubicle at the Aeolian Hall, which was soon thick
> with cigarette smoke. I had the score with me, and as the records
> were played he marked it wherever there was an effect or a tempo
> that he wanted altered. It was very interesting. He is most precise –
> he knows exactly what he wants – how, in his mind, that quartet,
> every bar of it, ought to sound. So armed with such final authority,
> we had another recording at the studio and my colleagues and I
> rehearsed hard for it over those little details. In recording we were
> very particular, with a metronome and a tuning fork, to get the
> tempo and pitch exactly right. [...] Ravel subsequently agreed that
> the new reading of the Quartet could be called a 'version de l'auteur'
> saying: 'It will constitute a real document for posterity to consult,
> and through gramophone records composers can now say definitely
> how they meant their works to be performed.' [2]

Ravel may have been meticulous but one thing he did not

[2] Mangeot, André, 'The Ravel String Quartet', *The Gramophone*, September 1927.
Reprinted in *The Gramophone Jubilee Book, 1923-1973* (General Gramophone Publications Ltd., 1973), pp. 60-63.

bother to mark was the essential *portamento* with which his music ought to be played. The same is true of Bartók, another immensely finicky composer. Although it is easy today to find ill-informed people who think it is tasteless to make any sort of slide, it never occurred to either Ravel or Bartók that a day would come when string players would not do slides. (There is, for example, a violin theme in the first movement of Ravel's Piano Trio which sounds naked and tasteless without a downward *portamento*.) In the International Quartet's recording the right style can be heard, delivered by a good but not great ensemble, playing on gut strings. The players judge the slowing down at the end of the opening movement very well. At the start of the scherzo-like second movement the *pizzicato* rhythm is almost pedantic, suggesting that Ravel laid great stress on getting the rhythm right at the start of the movement, and the slower sections are languorous without ever becoming static, as so many modern interpretations do. On the other hand, later in the performance there are little faults of intonation which seem not to have bothered Ravel much, so perhaps even he was more interested in getting the spirit right.

The 1934 recording, made in Paris by the Galimir Quartet of Vienna (Felix Galimir and his sisters Adrienne, Renée and Marguerite) and also supervised by the composer, shows many similarities with the 1927 performance, notably in the almost dogged accuracy of the *pizzicati* at the start of the second movement. The playing is lovely and technically often superior to that of the International Quartet, especially in intonation. By 1934 Ravel was in poor health, however, and although everyone agrees that he tended to revive when working with musicians on his music, this recording, for all its merits, is not the equal of its predecessor. In particular, the first movement is taken too fast for comfort. Not surprisingly, when Felix Galimir came to record the work again almost half a century later, he adopted a basic tempo for this movement even fractionally slower than that of the International Quartet. Timings are not in themselves reliable guides to performances but in this case the timings for the *Allegro moderato* tell a significant tale – International Quartet : 7' 26"; Galimir I: 6' 34"; Galimir II: 7' 45". To my mind, the International Quartet better captures the brightly-lit atmosphere of the *Très lent* third movement, in which Ravel was surely thinking of the brilliant sunlight of the Basque country, where his mother came from. Reference to the other recordings mentioned will show that they have much in common, both with each other and with the two composer-supervised performances.

ERNEST BLOCH (1880-1959)

There ought to be at least *some* British involvement in this exercise and the obvious relationship to focus on, it seems to me, is that between Ernest Bloch and the Griller Quartet. Today Bloch, born in Switzerland and a violin pupil of Ysaÿe among others, is not a fashionable figure. He is best known for the music reflecting his Jewish background and in fact his First Quartet, a massive work almost an hour long and written in 1916 when he was a mature artist of thirty-six, is in this mode. He did not complete another quartet until 1945, and it seems to have been inspired by the friendship with the Griller Quartet, which resulted in the production of three more works in the early 1950s.

The players – three Britons and a South African – got to know Bloch before the Second World War, when they were asked to perform the First Quartet both for a BBC broadcast and at the inaugural concert of the Bloch Society at the Aeolian Hall on 19 December 1937. The connection with the composer was made by Alex Cohen, former leader of the City of Birmingham Orchestra and one of Sidney Griller's mentors (and incidentally the dedicatee of the Second Quartet). After the war, when both ensemble and composer were based in the United States, the relationship deepened until the Grillers became Bloch's favourite interpreters. With his knowledge of string playing, he did not need to use them as laboratory helpers, but they undoubtedly sparked off his creative urge. He assisted them in preparing all his quartets and he supervised the recordings they made. After the final rehearsal for the premiere of the Second, he said: "It is a composer's dream come true to hear his work played as you have played it."[3] The Grillers also gave many performances of the two piano quintets and a private tape of the Second Quintet is in the Griller family collection.

The heroic Griller performance of the First Quartet is, I think, among the twenty or so greatest string quartet records (with the

[3] Quoted in the programme note for the first performance in Boston, Mass., 5 March 1947.

Second not far behind), but if I had to choose just one excerpt to show off the Grillers' playing, it would be the slow movement of the more concise Fourth Quartet, composed in 1953 and premiered by the ensemble in London in January 1954. The Fourth may be more modest than the first three quartets but it is quite dramatic in places, with touches of atonality and 12-note writing. In the Griller performance the tempo relationships are exemplary, so that each movement retains its distinct character. The *andante* speaks for itself but it shows the players' total immersion in the music and their fine technical control. The Griller Quartet was a very modern ensemble in that – despite Sidney Griller's dominant personality – it was particularly well balanced, with all four parts always well in the picture. This approach, with each player pulling his weight at all times, served Bloch well. Certainly he has been nowhere near as well interpreted by the few subsequent ensembles that have played his music.

BÉLA BARTÓK (1881-1945)

Alas, we have no records of the old Hungarian Quartet, known at home as the Waldbauer-Kerpély Quartet, which worked closely with Béla Bartók and Zoltán Kodály from 1910 to the mid-1930s. Nor are we well off for historic documents of the Bartók quartets in general. The Quatuor Pro Arte, who had a certain amount of contact with the composer, recorded the First Quartet but the work is not of much interest and, in any case, the Pro Arte's real Bartók warhorse was the Fourth Quartet. The Budapest and Amar Quartets recorded the Second Quartet, but neither of them particularly impressively, and so it is probably more profitable to concentrate on the Fifth Quartet. Five recordings of this work have claims to historical authenticity: one by the Kolisch Quartet, who gave the premiere, and two each by the Végh Quartet and the group known at first as the New Hungarian Quartet. The Kolisch version, which was not published at the time, is somewhat strange. By the time it was made, only the violinists were left of the players who had given the first performance and, although this new Kolisch Quartet was actually better balanced than the original, it did not chime well with Bartók's music. The New Hungarian Quartet gave most of the early performances, at first under Sándor Végh's leadership and then with him as second violin and Zoltán Székely as leader. Végh left at the end of 1938 and in 1940 formed his own quartet, with which he recorded the work in 1956 and 1972; both versions bear the imprint of his work with the composer on the score. Székely was a close friend and colleague of Bartók and first studied the Fifth Quartet with three partners in the New Hungarian Quartet who had been through the music with the composer not long before. In 1946 he and his colleagues, by then called simply the Hungarian Quartet, recorded the work and in 1961, after two more personnel changes, they recorded it again.

One might think that Végh's 1956 LP and the Hungarians' 1946 78 rpm discs would be more authentic than their remakes but, to my ears, the reverse is true. The Végh Quartet could be very slovenly and owed its reputation to its leader's amazing musical personality. In the early 1970s the group pulled itself together and concentrated for long enough to set down excellent Beethoven and Bartók cycles. Nevertheless for the Fifth Quartet I would recommend the 1961 Hungarian Quartet's performance because their recorded cycle is the finest all-round that we have had. In the 1940s and 1950s, they had a Russian-trained second violinist and a rather dominant cellist. By 1961 all the members were from similar backgrounds and the balance was better. Besides Székely, they still included the original violist, Dénes Koromzay – the man who had originally borrowed the manuscript score of the Fifth Quartet from his former teacher Imre Waldbauer, leader of the old Hungarian Quartet:

> One evening I went to Waldbauer's home with Pál Kadosa to play bridge. When I entered his living room I saw that there on the piano lay a new Bartók manuscript. […] 'What is this?' I asked. Waldbauer replied: 'Bela just sent over his Fifth Quartet. We have to learn it.' So I said to him: 'Could you loan me the score for just a very short time?' He agreed. 'There is no hurry for us so you can have it for two days.' […] Immediately phone calls went out to our friends Sándor Veress and Pál Kadosa, young composers at that time […] they came practically in pyjamas in ten minutes, and tore open the score. One took three movements and the other took two, and they went home and copied it. Later we put the score together again and dutifully took it back to Waldbauer, saying nothing. […] We worked very hard, and after three or four weeks we called Bartók and asked whether he would like to hear it. […] So we played it for him and […] he worked with us every day for ten days, after which he said: 'You can play the first performance in Budapest.'[4]

[4] Kenneson, Claude, *Székely and Bartók: The Story of a Friendship* (Portland, Oregon: Amadeus Press, 1994), p. 169.

The Hungarian Quartet's performance is beautifully and sympathetically played, with superb timing and pacing. It is also the only interpretation which makes me laugh (and this is Bartók's most humorous quartet). The humour tells particularly in the last two movements – the 'café band' interlude in the finale is done with a delightfully tongue-in-cheek insouciance. As a bonus, the entire cycle is very well recorded and has been transferred successfully to CD. I would not want to be without the Végh Quartet's somewhat shaggier performance but the Hungarian Bartók cycle is one of those miraculous recorded monuments that crop up only every so often. In all six works the performances have a naturalness and 'rightness' that put some over-praised more recent cycles firmly in their place.

ALBAN BERG (1885-1935)

The Galimir Quartet of Vienna was as meticulous as the Kolisch Quartet in seeking out living composers and asking their advice before playing their music. If, in the case of Ravel, the result was somewhat equivocal, the ensemble did score palpable hits with Darius Milhaud and Alban Berg. Milhaud supervised the Galimir recording of his Seventh Quartet in 1935 which, although hardly an immense challenge to the players or even one of the composer's more significant works, can be recommended wholeheartedly.

The *Lyric Suite* by Berg is a different matter. From the beginning it has been regarded as a masterpiece and whereas the stock of Berg's teacher Schoenberg has fallen, that of Berg himself has steadily risen. When the young Galimir siblings sought him out, they were still students at the Vienna Conservatory; but he was impressed by their commitment to his music and sat in on a number of their rehearsals of the *Lyric Suite*, offering comments, suggestions and encouragement. Had his life not been cut short by septicaemia in December 1935, he would presumably have been asked to supervise their 1936 recording. As it is, the performance is the only one we have by an ensemble which was coached by the composer. Galimir himself also left us a later recording with different colleagues, a performance which is similar in outline to the 1936 recording but slightly more expansive in all the movements except the first and last: this later recording has, of course, a much better sound, with a better dynamic range, and reflects almost half a century of further performances of the music. Its air of wisdom and intellectual penetration cannot be gainsaid. Nevertheless, there is something special about the 1936 recording. For one thing, the style of the playing is exactly what Berg would have expected to hear: it is light and airy in the Viennese way, with delightful touches of *portamento* – very similar to the style of the work's original performers the Kolisch Quartet, in fact, only rather more accomplished. There was no way in which Galimir could have instilled this style into his Japanese and American partners of the 1980s. The 1936 recording stands as a precious memento of its age. The way the Galimirs handle the alternations of fast and slow movements is masterly; proportion is everything in this work, but the players must also find the right atmosphere for each movement. The fugitive scurryings of the *Allegro misterioso* are particularly well captured and throughout the work the internal balance of the four parts is well conveyed by the recording.

DMITRI SHOSTAKOVICH (1906-1975)

The Beethoven Quartet was formed in 1923 (as the Moscow Conservatory Quartet) and went forty-one years without a change in personnel. These four players were influential in Soviet music in all sorts of ways. The leader Dmitri Tsyganov was not only a virtuoso but a remarkable musician; the second violinist Vassily Shirinsky was a composer, a musicologist, an excellent fiddler and a close friend of Dmitri Shostakovich; the violist Vadim Borisovsky was the father of the Russian viola school; and the cellist Sergei Shirinsky, Vassily's brother, was one of the supreme quartet cellists. They gave countless premieres and had many works dedicated to them but their most lasting and far-reaching collaboration was with Shostakovich, a collaboration which began just after the First Quartet had been premiered by the Glazunov Quartet of St. Petersburg in 1938. The Beethoven Quartet asked for the music and prepared it diligently but when Shostakovich heard them play, he remarked that their tempi were all wrong. It transpired that his watch had not been working properly and so the metronome marks were adrift. This embarrassing encounter was the start of a real friendship. There are many interesting things about the quartet's interaction with the composer in Elizabeth Wilson's fascinating book *Shostakovich: A Life Remembered* and elsewhere. Tsyganov, the leader of the Beethoven Quartet, remembers "the gentleness and unobtrusiveness of Shostakovich's observations [behind which] lay a profound sense of conviction concerning everything which touched upon the problems of interpreting his works".[5] The writer Aitmatov, invited by the composer to hear the new Fourteenth Quartet being rehearsed, on the other hand, recalled "some kind of mercilessly exacting force" which

> had awakened in him, a force which exerted itself both on himself and others. [...] Heaven knows, the musicians had played excellently, not merely with intelligence and feeling but giving their whole being to the music they were performing. [...] But the composer demanded more skill, more precision, more inspiration. He even complained to one of the players that he was breathing too audibly as he moved his bow. He had been associated with this quartet for years – more than thirty years of artistic collaboration. Yet how strict he was with them! [...] I listened and marvelled: so that's the kind of man you are! Gentle, good-hearted, diffident Shostakovich – but a wild beast when it comes to work! [6]

The Beethoven Quartet's performances always seem to me to be very faithful and yet quite free, in the sense that the players do to the music what any good musicians ought to do, without making obvious points all the time. They also avoid the mannerisms which disfigure many of the Borodin Quartet's performances. Their recordings are full of amazing playing, not least Tsyganov's heroic handling of the *Recitative* in the Second Quartet, a work they recorded for both Melodiya and Supraphon. But of the discs made by the original members, that of the best-known quartet, the Eighth, is as representative as any, especially as the recording was made in 1961, quite soon after the premiere. Since the controversy of *Testimony*,[7] this work has been burdened with all manner of interpretations and counter-interpretations which may (or may not) be relevant. The 'Beethoveners', with only Shostakovich's original anti-Fascist programme to go on (unless they were privy to autobiographical revelations at their coaching sessions with him), give a reading of unique power, concentration and inwardness. The technical quality of the playing, while never showy, is also magnificent.

---

[5] Sollertinsky, Dmitri and Ludmilla, *Pages from the Life of Dmitri Shostakovich* (London: Robert Hale 1981), pp. 219-220.
[6] *Ibid.*, pp. 220-221.
[7] Shostakovich, Dmitri, *Testimony*, as related to and edited by Solomon Volkov, trans. Antonia W. Bouis, (New York: Harper and Row Publishers Inc., 1979).

VAGN HOLMBOE (1909-1996)

It is impossible in a book of this size to discuss every twentieth-century quartet composer but I would like to register a personal plea for the Danish composer Vagn Holmboe who wrote twenty quartets, as well as a concerto for quartet and orchestra, and left at least ten quartets unfinished along the way. He was influenced by Bartók to start with but gradually found his own voice, using elements of folk music in many of his works. In my view, his quartet cycle is of immense importance and the recently-completed series of recordings by the excellent Kontra Quartet is to be welcomed. Beginning with the Seventh Quartet, written in 1964 and 1965, Holmboe collaborated closely with the Copenhagen Quartet, whose leader Tutter Givskov is very much alive and still passing on her lifetime's accumulation of experience to students. This is what she had to say about Holmboe in a letter to me:

> Our work with his quartets took place as follows: first we received a new quartet, then we rehearsed it and finally, a week before we had to play it in concert, we invited Holmboe to hear the result. He sat there with his score and we expected him to correct a few things, e.g. the tempi or the phrasing, but he was always satisfied with our performance even though it didn't always match his metronome indications and nuances. 'Pay no attention to that,' he said; our interpretation was exactly what he had had in mind. Gradually we had become familiar with his language of tones, so it didn't seem hard to play his pieces. He made a point of his music being played very accurately and clearly, in such a way that all parts would be heard and his intentions with the piece would be clearer. In particular, it was hard to play the third movement of no. 8 (with all the triplets – which he used very often) in a clear and transparent way. He never participated in editing the recording but left it entirely up to us, and was very pleased with the result.[8]

Founded in 1957, the Copenhagen Quartet had a career of thirty-eight years with only one personnel change in 1974, when the second violinist Mogens Lydolph became ill and had to withdraw. His replacement was Mogens Durholm, concertmaster of the Royal Orchestra. The group played all twenty of Holmboe's quartets in concert but recorded only the first eight (with Lydolph) and nos. 15 and 16 (with Durholm). The recording of the Eighth

---

[8] Undated letter to the author, autumn 1999.

Quartet, with that tricky third movement mentioned in Tutter Givskov's letter, was made by the original ensemble and is a good illustration of their work. The Eighth Quartet was written in 1965 and Holmboe saw it as forming a pair with the Seventh Quartet. The third movement, *Presto colante e robusto*, is a short and brilliant scherzo which stands at the centre of a Bartókian arch form of five movements. The entire performance enhances one's admiration of the Copenhagen players, who – like Holmboe himself – have been seriously underrated. Perhaps because they were based in Scandinavia, they never attracted much publicity, but their recordings of the late Beethoven quartets show their sterling qualities and they bring the same attributes of rhythmic zest and structural sense to the Holmboe quartets, as well as their fine technical command and feeling for tone colour. It is to be hoped that some of their records of his music will appear on CD, as the five performances known to me have exceptional authority.

RECORDINGS CONSIDERED

Reger: Quartet no. 4 in E flat, op. 109
Recommended performance: Busch Quartet (Adolf Busch, Bruno Straumann, Hugo Gottesmann, Herman Busch), Bavarian Radio 224767/9, rec. 15 February 1951, Munich; reissued on Brüder-Busch-Gesellschaft LP and Eastworld (Japan) CD SCR-8520.
Also considered: Strub Quartet (Max Strub, Jost Raba, Walter Trampler, Ludwig Hoelscher), HMV EH-1264/7, rec. May 1935 and June 1938; reissued on Eastworld (Japan) CD SGR-8509. Drolc Quartet (Eduard Drolc, Jürgen Paarmann, Stefano Passaggio, Georg Donderer), Deutsche Grammophon LP 139438, rec. 14-18 April 1969, Berlin.

Suk: Quartet no. 1 in B flat, op. 11
Recommended performance: Bohemian Quartet (Karel Hoffman, Josef Suk, Jiří Herold, Ladislav Zelenka), Polydor 95076/9, rec. 1928; reissued on Biddulph CDs LAB-091/2.

Schoenberg: Quartet no. 4 op. 37
Recommended performance: Kolisch Quartet (Rudolf Kolisch, Felix Khuner, Eugen Lehner, Benar Heifetz), private discs, rec. 8 January 1937, Hollywood; reissued on Archiphon CDs ARC-103/4.

Ravel: Quartet in F
Recommended performance: International Quartet (André Mangeot, Boris Pecker, Frank Howard, Herbert Withers), National Gramophonic Society NGS78/81, rec. June 1927, London; reissued on Music & Arts CD-703.
Also considered: Galimir Quartet I (Felix, Adrienne, Renée and Marguerite Galimir), Polydor 516758/60, rec. 1934, Paris: reissued on Rockport RR5007. Galimir Quartet II (Felix Galimir, Hiroko Yajima, John Graham, Timothy Eddy), Vanguard CD 25009, rec. c1982, New York.

Bloch: Quartet no. 4
Recommended performance: Griller Quartet (Sidney Griller, Jack O'Brien, Philip Burton, Colin Hampton), Decca LP LXT-5073, rec. c1955, London.

Bartók: Quartet no. 5 Sz. 102
Recommended performance: Hungarian Quartet (Zoltán Székely, Michael Kuttner, Dénes Koromsay, Gabriel Magyar), Deutsche Grammophon LP SLMP-138 650/2, rec. 1961, Hanover; reissued on Deutsche Grammophon 'The Originals' CDs 457 740-2.
Also considered: Végh Quartet (Sándor Végh, Sándor Zöldy, Georges Janzer, Paul Szabo), Telefunken LP SKH-25083, rec. 1972, La Chaux-de-Fonds; reissued on Auvidis Astrée CD E-7719.

Berg: *Lyric Suite*
Recommended performance: Galimir Quartet I (Felix, Adrienne, Renée and Marguerite Galimir), Polydor 516659/62, rec. 1936, Paris; reissued on Continuum CD SBT-1004 and Rockport CD RR-5007.
Also considered: Galimir Quartet II (Felix Galimir, Hiroko Yajima, John Graham, Timothy Eddy), Vanguard CD 08-9198-71, rec. c1983, New York.

Shostakovich: Quartet no. 8 op. 110
Recommended performance: Beethoven Quartet (Dmitri Tsyganov, Vassily Shirinsky, Vadim Borisovsky, Sergei Shirinsky), Melodiya LP 08019/20, rec. 1961; reissued on Consonance CD 81-3006.

Holmboe: Quartet no. 8 op. 87
Recommended performance: Copenhagen Quartet (Tutter Givskov, Mogens Lydolph, Mogens Bruun, Asger Lund Christiansen), Vox Turnabout LP TV-34217S, rec. c1968, Copenhagen.

Chronology of Selected Works
referred to in the Text

YEAR	COMPOSER	WORK
1885	Chadwick	Quartet no. 3
1893	Debussy	Quartet in G minor
1896	Zemlinsky	Quartet no. 1
1897	Schoenberg	Quartet in D
1903	Weigl	Quartet no. 1
1904	Ravel	Quartet in F major
1905	Schoenberg	Quartet no. 1
1907/8		Quartet no. 2
1909	Bartók	Quartet no. 1
	Kodály	Quartet no. 1
	Reger	Quartet no. 2
	Suk	Quartet no. 1
	Webern	*Five Movements* op. 5
1910	Berg	Quartet op. 3
1911-13	Ives	Quartet no. 2
1913	Stravinsky	*Three Pieces*
	Webern	*Six Bagatelles* op. 9
1913/15	Zemlinsky	Quartet no. 2
1916	Bloch	Quartet no. 1
1917	Bartók	Quartet no. 2
	Martinů	Quartet in E flat
	Szymanowski	Quartet no. 1
1918	Hindemith	Quartet no. 1
	Kodály	Quartet no. 2
	Martinů	Quartet no. 1
1919	Hába	Quartet no. 1
1920	Enescu	Quartet no. 1
	Gershwin	*Lullaby*
	Hába	Quartet no. 2
	Stravinsky	*Concertino*
1922	Hába	Quartets nos. 3-4
1922/3	Hindemith	Quartets nos. 2-4
1923	Janáček	Quartet no. 1 ('Kreutzer Sonata')
	Zemlinsky	Quartet no. 3
1924	Fauré	Quartet
1925	Martinů	Quartet no. 2
1925/6	Berg	*Lyric Suite*
1927	Bartók	Quartet no. 3
	Schoenberg	Quartet no. 3
	Szymanowski	Quartet no. 2
1928	Bartók	Quartet no. 4
	Copland	*Two Pieces*
	Janáček	Quartet no. 2 ('Intimate Letters')

1929	Martinů	Quartet no. 3
1930	Britten	Quartet no. 1 (*Quartettino*)
1931	Crawford-Seeger	Quartet
1933/4	Roussel	Quartet op. 45
1934	Bartók	Quartet no. 5
	Tippett	Quartet no. 1
1936	Barber	Quartet
	Cowell	Quartet no. 4 (*United Quartet*)
	Zemlinsky	Quartet no. 4
1936/7	Honegger	Quartet
1937	Bridge	Quartet no. 4
	Martinů	Quartet no. 4
1938	Bacewicz	Quartet no. 1
	Martinů	Quartet no. 5
	Shostakovich	Quartet no. 1
	Webern	Quartet op. 28
1939	Bartók	Quartet no. 6
	Schuman	Quartet no. 3
1941	Prokofiev	Quartet no. 2
1942	Tippett	Quartet no. 2
1943	Ullmann	Quartet no. 3
1944	Shostakovich	Quartet no. 2
1945	Bloch	Quartet no. 2
	Britten	Quartet no. 2
1946	Bacewicz	Quartet no. 3
	Martinů	Quartet no. 6
	Shostakovich	Quartet no. 3
	Zemlinsky	Quartet no. 4
1947	Henze	Quartet no. 1
1948	Maconchy	Quartet no. 5
1948-9	Boulez	*Livre pour Quatuor*
1949	Shostakovich	Quartet no. 4
1950	Hába	Quartet no. 6
1951	Bacewicz	Quartet no. 4
	Carter	Quartet no. 1
	Enescu	Quartet no. 2
	Hába	Quartets nos. 7-8
	Sessions	Quartet no. 2
1952	Lutyens	Quartet no. 6
	Seiber	*Quartetto Lirico*
	Shostakovich	Quartet no. 5
1953	Bloch	Quartet no. 4
	Piston	Quartet no. 4
1954	Ligeti	Quartet no. 1
1955	Bacewicz	Quartet no. 5
1956	Shostakovich	Quartet no. 6
1957	Shostakovich	Quartet no. 7
1959	Carter	Quartet no. 2
	Kurtág	Quartet no. 1
1960	Bacewicz	Quartet no. 6

1960	Penderecki	Quartet no. 1
	Shostakovich	Quartet no. 8
1963	Hába	Quartet no. 14
	Ohana	Cinq séquences
1964	Hába	Quartet no. 15
	Lutosławski	Quartet
1965	Bacewicz	Quartet no. 7
	Holmboe	Quartets nos. 7-8
	Maw	Quartet no. 1
1966	Jolas	Quartet no. 2
	Schnittke	In Memoriam Igor Stravinsky
1968	Boucourechliev	Archipel II
	Ligeti	Quartet no. 2
	Penderecki	Quartet no. 2
1970	Crumb	Black Angels
1971	Wood	Quartet no. 2
1972	Gilbert	String Quartet with Piano Pieces
1973	Shostakovich	Quartet no. 14
1974		Quartet no. 15
1976	Dutilleux	Ainsi la nuit
	Ferneyhough	Sonatas
	Goehr	Quartet no. 3
	Panufnik	Quartet no. 1
1976-7	Henze	Quartets nos. 3-5
1977	Kurtág	12 Microludes
1980	Ferneyhough	Quartet no. 2
	Panufnik	Quartet no. 2
1981	Kurtág	Aus der Ferne I
1982	Dusapin	Quartet no. 1
	Gilbert	Quartets nos. 2-3
1983	Cage	30 Pieces for String Quartet
	Glass	Quartet no. 2 ('Company')
	Lumsdaine	Mandala IV
	Martinů	Quartet
	Schnittke	Quartet no. 3
	Xenakis	Tetras
1984	Finnissy	Quartet
1986	Kurtág	Aus der Ferne II
1987	Gilbert	Quartet no. 3
	Gubaidulina	Quartet no. 3
1988	Butler	Quartet no. 3
	Górecki	Quartet no. 1 ('Already it is dusk')
	LeFanu	Quartet no. 1
1988/9	Dusapin	Quartet no. 2 ('Time Zones')
1989	Holt	Danger of the Disappearance of Things
1990	Panufnik	Quartet no. 3
1991	Górecki	Quartet no. 2 (Quasi una fantasia)
	Kurtág	Aus der Ferne III
1992	Dusapin	Quartet no. 3
1995	Carter	Quartet no. 5

Select Bibliography

I – THE AUSTRO-GERMAN QUARTET

Adorno, Theodor W., *Alban Berg*, trans. Julianne Brand and Christopher
  Hailey (Cambridge: Cambridge University Press, 1991)
Frisch, Walter, *The Early Works of Arnold Schoenberg, 1893-1908* (Berkeley:
  University of California Press, 1993)
Hailey, Christopher, 'Berg and the Viennese Dichotomy' in Jarman, Douglas
  (ed.), *The Berg Companion* (London: Macmillan, 1989)
—— 'Schoenberg and the Canon; an Evolving Heritage', in Hailey, C. and
  Brand, J., *Constructive Dissonance* (Berkeley: University of California Press,
  1997)
Henze, Hans Werner, in the notes to the recording of the complete Henze
  String Quartets by the Arditti Quartet (WER 60114/15-50).
Hinton, Stephen, 'Germany 1918-1945' in Morgan, Robert (ed.), *Man and
  Music: Modern Times* (London: Macmillan, 1993)
Keller, Hans, 'Schoenberg and the Crisis of Communication' in *The London
  Sinfonietta Schoenberg/Gerhard Series* (London: Sinfonietta Productions
  Ltd., 1973)
Moldenhauer, Hans, *Anton von Webern*, (London: Gollancz, 1978)
Perle, George, 'The Secret Programme of the Lyric Suite', *Musical Times*,
  1314-1616, 1977
Puffett, Derrick, [critique of Berg's analysis in] ' "Music that lingers within
  one" for a Lifetime', *Music and Letters*, 76/ii, May 1995
Rauchhaupt, Ursula von, *Schoenberg, Berg, Webern: the string quartets, a
  documentary study* (Hamburg: Deutsche Grammophon Gesellschaft, 1971)
Schmidt, Christian Martin, 'Schoenberg's "Very Definite but Private"
  Programm zum Streichquartett op. 7' in *Bericht über den 2 Kongress der
  Internationalen Schoenberg-Gesellschaft* (Wien: Verlag Elisabeth Lafite,
  1986)
Schoenberg, Arnold, 'Brahms the Progressive' in *Style and Idea* (London:
  Faber and Faber, 1984)
Smith, Joan Allen, *Schoenberg and his School*, (New York: Schirmer, 1986)
Stravinsky in Conversation with Robert Craft (Harmondsworth: Penguin, 1962)
Webern, Anton, *The Path to New Music* (Pennsylvania: Theodor Presser and
  Co., 1963)

II – THE FRENCH QUARTET

Bayer, Francis, *De Schönberg à Cage: essai sur la notion d'espace sonore dans la
  musique contemporaine* (Paris: Klinksieck, 2/1987)
Boulez, Pierre, *Conversations with Célestin Deliège*, (London: Eulenberg, 1976)
Goldet, Stéphane, *Quatuors du XXe siècle* (Paris: IRCAM-Papiers, 1987)

Jameux, Dominique, *Boulez* (Paris: Fayard, 1984)
Jones, John Barrie (ed. and trans.), *Gabriel Fauré: a Life in Letters* (London, Batsford, 1989)
Lesure, François and Nichols, Roger (eds.), *Debussy Letters* (London: Faber, 1987)
Nattiez, Jean-Jacques (ed.), *The Boulez-Cage Correspondence* (Cambridge: Cambridge University Press, 1993)
Nichols, Roger, *Ravel* (London: Dent, 1977)
—— Interview with Dutilleux on 11 April 1991. Part of this interview was published in the *Musical Times* in February 1994
Orledge, Robert, *Gabriel Fauré*, 2nd edn, (London: Eulenberg, 1983)
Poirier, Alain, 'Le quatuor à cordes après 1945, entre le genre et le médium instrumental' in *Le quatuor à cordes en France de 1750 à nos jours*
Potter, Caroline, *Henri Dutilleux: His Life and Works* (Aldershot: Ashgate, 1997)
Roy, Jean, 'Les quatuors de Fauré, Debussy, Ravel et Roussel' in *Le quatuor à cordes en France de 1750 à nos jours* (Paris: Association Française pour la Patrimoine Nationale, 1995)

III – THE CENTRAL EUROPEAN QUARTET

Bayley, Amanda (ed.), *The Cambridge Companion to Bartók* (Cambridge: Cambridge University Press, 2001)
Eősze, László, *Zoltán Kodály. His Life and Work*, trans. István Farkas and Gyula Gulyás (London: Collet's, 1962)
Gillies, Malcolm (ed.), *The Bartók Companion* (London: Faber and Faber, 1993)
Griffiths, Paul, *György Ligeti* (London: Robson Books, 1983)
Hollander, Hans, *Leoš Janáček. His Life and Work*, trans. Paul Hamburger (London: John Calder, 1963)
Jacobson, Bernard, *A Polish Renaissance* (London: Phaidon Press, 1996)
Kaczyński, Tadeusz, *Conversations with Witold Lutosławski* (London: Chester, 1984)
Kárpáti, János, *Bartók's Chamber Music*, trans. Fred MacNicol and Mária Steiner, trans. rev. Paul Merrick (New York: Pendragon Press, 1994)
Lang, Paul Henry and Broder, Nathan (eds.), *Contemporary Music in Europe: A Comprehensive Survey* (New York: Schirmer, 1965)
Ligeti, György with Péter Varnai, Josef Häuser and Claude Samuel, *Ligeti in Conversation* (London: Eulenberg Books, 1983)
Malcolm, Noel, *George Enescu: His Life and Music* (London: Toccata Press, 1990)
Nordwall, Ove (ed.), *Lutosławski*, trans. Christoper Gibbs.(Stockholm: Edition Wilhelm Hansen, 1968).
Rae, Charles Bodman, *The Music of Lutosławski* (London: Omnibus Press, 1999)
Rappoport-Gelfand, Lidia, *Musical Life in Poland: The Postwar Years 1945-1977*, trans. Irina Lasoff (New York: Gordon and Breach, 1991)
Rosen, Judith, *Grażyna Bacewicz: Her Life and Works*. Polish Music History Series Vol. 2. (Los Angeles: Friends of Polish Music, 1984)
Sadie, Stanley (ed.), *The New Grove Dictionary of Music and Musicians* (London: Macmillan, 2001)
Šafránek, Miloš, *Bohuslav Martinů: His Life and Works*, trans. Roberta Finlayson-Samsourová (London: Allan Wingate, 1962)
Samson, Jim, *The Music of Szymanowski* (London: Kahn and Averill, 1981)

Schwinger, Wolfram, *Krzysztof Penderecki. His Life and Work: Encounters, Biography and Musical Commentary*, trans. William Mann (London: Schott, 1989)

Stevens, Halsey, *The Life and Music of Béla Bartók*, 3rd edn, ed. Malcolm Gillies (Oxford: Clarendon Press, 1993)

Stucky, Stephen, *Lutosławski and His Music* (Cambridge: Cambridge University Press, 1981)

Suchoff, Benjamin (ed.), *Béla Bartók Essays* (London: Faber and Faber, 1976; repr. Lincoln, Nebr., and London: University of Nebraska Press, 1992)

Varga, Bálint András, *Lutosławski Profile* (London: Chester, 1976)

Vogel, Jaroslav, *Leoš Janáček: A Biography* (London: Orbis, 1981)

Walsh, Stephen, 'György Kurtág: an outline study (I)', *Tempo*, no. 140, March 1982, pp. 11-21

Wightman, Alistair, *Karol Szymanowski:His Life and Work* (Aldershot: Ashgate, 1999)

Willson, Rachel Beckles, 'Kurtág's Instrumental Music, 1988-1998', *Tempo*, no. 207, December 1998

Zaimont, Judith Lang, Overhause, Catherine and Gottlieb, Jane (eds.), *The Musical Woman: An International Perspective*, (Westport: Greenwood Press, 1984)

IV – THE SOVIET AND RUSSIAN QUARTET

Griffiths, Paul, *The String Quartet – A History* (London: Thames & Hudson, 1983)

Rowland, Christopher and George, Alan, in *Shostakovich: the Man and His Music*, ed. Christopher Norris (London: Lawrence and Wishart Ltd., 1982)

V –THE BRITISH QUARTET

Evans, P., 'Sonata Structures in early Britten', *Tempo*, no. 82, 1967

Harries, Merrion & Susan, *A Pilgrim Soul: The Life and Work of Elisabeth Lutyens* (London: Michael Joseph, 1989)

Hill, P., 'Tippett's Fifth String Quartet', *Tempo*, no. 192, 1991

Keller, H., 'Benjamin Britten's Second Quartet', *Tempo*, no. 18, 1947

Kemp, I. (ed.), *Michael Tippett: a Symposium on his 60th Birthday* (London: Eulenberg, 1965)

—— *Tippett: The Composer and his Music* (London: Eulenberg, 1984)

LeFanu, N., 'David Lumsdaine', *Musical Times*, cxvii, 1976

Matthews, D., *Michael Tippett: an Introductory Study* (London: Faber and Faber, 1980)

Matthew-Walker, R., 'The Early String Quartets of Elizabeth Maconchy', *Musical Opinion*, cxii, 1989

Mellers, W., 'Michael Tippett and the String Quartet', *The Listener*, lxvi, 1961

Mitchell, D. and Keller, H. (eds.), *Benjamin Britten: a Commentary on his Works from a Group of Specialists* (London: Faber and Faber, 1952)

Northcott, B., 'Nicholas Maw', *Music and Musicians*, xviii/9, 1970

—— (ed.), *The Music of Alexander Goehr* (London: Schott & Co., 1980)

Payne, A. and Foreman, L., *The Music of Frank Bridge* (London: Thames

Publishing, 1976)

Puffett, D., 'The Fugue from Tippett's Second String Quartet', *Music Analysis*, v, 1986

—— (ed.) *Finding the Key: Selected Writings of Alexander Goehr* (London: Faber and Faber, 1998)

Schultz, A., 'Identity and Memory: Temporality in the Music of David Lumsdaine', *Studies in Music* (Austr.), xxv, 1991

Seabrook, M. ' "Dark Fire": Simon Holt and his Music', *Tempo*, no. 201, 1997

Whittall, A. 'Maw's Instrumental Music', *Tempo*, no. 106, (1973)

—— 'Nicholas Maw' in Foreman, L. (ed.), *British Music Now* (London: 1975)

Whitehead, N. B. T., *Analytical Studies of the Work of Simon Holt* (Cambridge University Ph.D. thesis, 1997)

'Wood's Second Quartet' in *The Listener*, lxxxiv, 1970

VI –THE AMERICAN QUARTET

Block, Adrienne Fried, 'Boston Talks Back to Dvořák' in *Newsletter of the Institute for Studies in American Music*, 18/2, May 1989

Burkholder, J. Peter, *All Made of Tunes: Charles Ives and the Uses of Musical Borrowing* (New Haven, CT: Yale University Press, 1995)

Cowell, Henry, 'Trends in American Music' in *American Composers on American Music: A Symposium* (ed. Cowell), (New York: Frederick Ungar Publishing Co., 1961 [1933])

—— 'Towards Neo-Primitivism' in *Modern Music*, 10/3, 1933

—— [Introductory notes to the] *United Quartet* (San Francisco: New Music Edition, 1937)

Elliott Carter: In Conversation with Enzo Restagno for Settembre Musica 1989, trans. Katherine Siberblatt Wolfthal, I.S.A.M. Monograph no. 32, (Brooklyn, New York: Institute for Studies in American Music, 1991)

Gershwin, George, 'The Relation of Jazz to American Music' in *American Composers on American Music* (details as above)

Gillespie, Don, (compiler and ed.), *George Crumb: Profile of a Composer* (New York: C. F. Peters Corporation, 1986)

Hitchcock, H. Wiley, *Music in the United States: A Historical Introduction*, 3rd edition, (Englewood Cliffs, NJ: Prentice Hall, 1988)

Malone, Bill C., *Southern Music / American Music* (Lexington: Kentucky University Press, 1979)

Nanry, Charles (ed.), *American Music – from Storyville to Woodstock* (New Brunswick, NJ: Transaction Books, 1972)

Nicholls, David (ed.), *The Cambridge History of American Music* (Cambridge: Cambridge University Press, 1998)

—— 'Henry Cowell's *United Quartet*' in *American Music*, 13/2 (Summer 1995)

Olmstead, Andrea, *Conversations with Roger Sessions* (Boston: Northeastern University Press, 1987)

Partch, Harry, *Genesis of a Music*, 2nd edition, enlarged, (New York: Da Capo Press, 1979)

Sadie, Stanley and Hitchcock, H. Wiley (eds.), *The New Grove Dictionary of*

American Music (London: Macmillan, 1986)

Sinclair, James B., *A Descriptive Catalogue of the Music of Charles Ives* (New Haven, CT: Yale University Press, 1999)

Tibbetts, John C. (ed.), *Dvořák in America, 1892-1895* (Portland, Or.: Amadeus Press, 1993)

Tischler, Barbara L., *An American Music: the Search for an American Musical Identity* (New York: Oxford University Press, 1986)

VII – FRONTIERS OF QUARTET TECHNIQUE

Baillot, Pierre, *L'Art du violin: nouvelle méthode* (Paris: 1834, trans. L. Goldberg as *The Art of the Violin*, Evanston, Ill.: 1991)

Corder, Frederick, 'Quartet' in Grove, George (ed.), *A Dictionary of Music and Musicians* (London: 1879-89), Vol. 3

Quantz, Johann Joachim, *Versuch einer Anweisung die Flöte traversiere zu spielen* (Berlin: 1752, trans. E. R. Reilly as *On Playing the Flute*, London and New York: 1966)

VIII – THE RECORDED LEGACY

Grüters, Otto, *Adolf Buschs Lebenslauf*, manuscript, Busch Archiv, Max Reger-Institut, Karlsruhe

Kenneson, Claude, *Székely and Bartók: The Story of a Friendship* (Portland, Oregon: Amadeus Press, 1994)

Mangeot, André, 'The Ravel String Quartet', *The Gramophone*, September 1927. Reprinted in *the Gramophone Jubilee Book, 1923-1973* (General Gramophone Publications Ltd., 1973)

Potter, Tully, *Adolf Busch: The Life of an Honest Musician* (London: Toccata Press, in preparation)

Shostakovich, Dmitri, *Testimony*, as related to and edited by Solomon Volkov, trans. Antonia W. Bouis, (New York: Harper and Row Publishers Inc., 1979)

Sollertinsky, Dmitri and Ludmilla, *Pages from the Life of Dmitri Shostakovich* (London: Robert Hale 1981)

Wilson, Elizabeth, *Shostakovich: A Life Remembered* (London: Faber and Faber, 1994)

About the Authors

AMANDA BAYLEY is Senior Lecturer in Music at the University of Wolverhampton. She has edited *The Cambridge Companion to Bartók* (Cambridge University Press, 2001) and has also published on Bartók's Fourth Quartet. She has received awards for post-doctoral research at the Budapest Bartók Archive and at the British Library National Sound Archive as an Edison Fellow. She is currently preparing a book on *Bartók Performance Studies*. Her research focuses on issues of notation in performance and analysis.

DUNCAN DRUCE, composer, violinist, lecturer and writer on music, gained a double first in music at Cambridge. He came to prominence as a performer in 1967 when he joined the Pierrot Players – later the Fires of London. As a founder-member of the Academy of Ancient Music and, with Alan Hacker, The Music Party, he became a notable pioneer of historically-informed performances of Baroque and Classical music. He now lives in West Yorkshire and combines performance and composition with teaching at Huddersfield University and Leeds University (Bretton Hall).

ALAN GEORGE studied at the Royal Academy of Music with Sidney Griller and at King's College Cambridge where he became a founder-member of the Fitzwilliam String Quartet. He has performed worldwide with the Quartet, and their many recordings include the first complete set of the fifteen Shostakovich quartets. Following the Quartet's residency at York University, he became a lecturer and Director of the Chamber Orchestra until 1988. Author of two studies of Shostakovich's chamber music and numerous articles, he is currently a tutor in viola and chamber music at the RNCM.

ANTHONY GILBERT studied with Seiber and Goehr, and later at Tanglewood with Schuller, and came to prominence in the 1960s with a series of virtuoso chamber works performed in international festivals. Larger works followed, including a symphony premiered at the 1973 Cheltenham International Festival. That year he commenced a long and fruitful period as principal teacher of composition at the RNCM – twenty-six years interrupted only by spells in Australia, a country he has grown to love greatly. He has now written some eighty works in a wide range of genres.

DOUGLAS JARMAN is Principal Lecturer in Academic Studies at the RNCM. Author of three books and some two dozen articles on the music of Alban Berg, his most recent publications are the new critical edition of the Berg Violin Concerto for the Alban Berg Gesamtausgabe and the three short volumes *Henze at the RNCM* (Arc, 1999), which he edited to mark the composer's visit to Manchester in 1998. His new critical edition of the Berg *Chamber Concerto* will be published by Universal Edition and the Alban Berg Stiftung later this year.

DAVID NICHOLLS was Professor of Music and Research Dean of the Faculty of Humanities at Keele University, before moving in summer 2000 to a Chair in Music at the University of Southampton. He is author of *American Experimental Music, 1890-1940* (CUP, 1990), and contributing editor of *The Whole World of Music: a Henry Cowell Symposium* (Harwood, 1997), *The Cambridge History of American Music* (CUP, 1998), and the *Cambridge Companion to John Cage* (CUP, 2002). He is also editor of the journal *American Music*.

CAROLINE POTTER is Senior Lecturer in Music at Kingston University. She studied French and Music at Keele University and later pursued graduate study at Liverpool University under the supervision of Professor Robert Orledge. A specialist in French music, she is the author of *Henri Dutilleux* (Ashgate, 1997), and is currently co-editing a book on French music since Berlioz, also for Ashgate. Other current projects include a book on Nadia and Lili Boulanger.

TULLY POTTER was born in Edinburgh in 1942 but spent his formative years in South Africa where he studied singing in Johannesburg with Leah Williams. He has been collecting records seriously since he was twelve and has made a special study of performing practice as revealed in historic recordings. He has contributed to many international musical journals, notably *The Strad*, and since 1997 has edited the *Classic Record Collector*. His biography of Adolf Busch is due to be published soon, and he is preparing a book on the great string quartet ensembles.

Index